HOME ORGANIZING
IDEA BOOK

HOME ORGANIZING
IDEA BOOK

JOANNE KELLAR BOUKNIGHT AND JOHN LOECKE

The Taunton Press

The Taunton Press
Inspiration for hands-on living®

The Taunton Press, Inc., 63 South Main Street, PO Box 5506, Newtown, CT 06470-5506
e-mail: tp@taunton.com

COVER PHOTOGRAPHERS: Front cover: (top row, left to right) ©Wendell T. Webber,
©Rob Karosis, ©Wendell T. Webber, ©Charles Register; (bottom row, left to right)
©Phillip Ennis, ©Wendell T. Webber, ©Phillip Ennis, ©Wendell T. Webber.
Back cover: (top photo) Todd Caverly, ©Brian Vanden Brink Photography; (bottom
row, left to right) ©Mark Samu/Samu Studios, John Rickard, ©The Taunton Press, Inc.,
©Wendell T. Webber, ©Eric Roth.

LIBRARY OF CONGRESS CATALOGING-IN-PUBLICATION DATA:

Bouknight, Joanne Kellar.
  Home organizing idea book / Joanne Kellar Bouknight and John Loecke.
    p. cm.
  ISBN-13: 978-1-56158-859-6
  ISBN-10: 1-56158-859-8
  1. Storage in the home. 2. Orderliness. I. Loecke, John. II. Title.
  TX309.B67 2006
  648'.8--dc22
                            2005033823

Printed in Singapore
10 9 8 7 6 5 4 3 2 1

The following manufacturers/names appearing in *Home Organizing Idea Book*
are trademarks: Bed, Bath & Beyond®, Better Homes and Gardens®, California
Closets®, Casabella®, ClosetMaid®, The Container Store®, Exposures®, Fiestaware®,
Filofax®, Freedon Bag®, Frontgate®, Ikea®, Kmart™, LEGO®, Levenger®, NARI®,
Parents®, Rev-A-Shelf®, Rubbermaid®, Stacks and Stacks™, Target®, Tupperware®,
and Velcro®

Contents

Contents *(continued)*

Introduction

ORGANIZING IDEA BOOK

When I mentioned to friends and family that I was writing a book on organizing, I was greeted with silence. Then came the jokes and the ribbing. Would writing such a book empty my apartment of the dozens of Chinese figurines that fill my many bookshelves? How could someone who couldn't bear to part with piles of old decorating magazines enlighten others on the art of order?

Simple, I replied, because for me, a well-ordered home has always been an obsession. And, yes, my Chinoiserie stands at perfect attention and my magazines are boxed and labeled. Organization is a topic that I've both studied extensively and practiced professionally, both in my career as an interior designer and in my work as a contributing home editor to a number of national magazines, including Parents® and Better Homes and Gardens®.

But obsessed though I may be with the art of organizing, I did feel the need for additional backup as I wrote this book. And what I learned from talking to friends and experts such as Jill Markiewicz, the owner of Closet Couture, a high-style New York-based organizing service, and

Lyn Peterson, an interior designer, mother of four, and all-around organizing guru, was that many of us (myself included) avoid tackling organizing projects because we know things will only get worse before they get better. But that's simply how the process works, and once you've accepted that, the rest is easy.

I also discovered that organizing is a process and not one that requires you to tackle the entire house in one

sweeping session. For this reason, you'll find that this book is arranged according to the various hot spots in the home, starting with the area inside the front door and continuing through to the garage. So if you're obsessed with closets as I am (I've not only said good riddance to wire hangers, but I've also coordinated the contents of mine by color), you'll know right where to look.

What are you waiting for? Get organized!

—John Loecke

HOME STORAGE IDEA BOOK

I watched a squirrel from my kitchen window this morning as it scuttled up a post, chomped madly on an acorn, dashed down the post, and zigzagged through the grass, looking for a place to bury the acorn. It took a few more bites, ran a few steps, stopped suddenly, dug a quick hole, and dropped in the acorn, scrabbling the soil and grass frantically across the top. "And you're going to remember where that one is next spring?" I said to the squirrel.

But, in truth, there was no good reason to feel smug; squirrels are not the only species rushing around looking for something stored months ago, somewhere. Take a March morning, the first day of spring soccer—when shin pads, soccer cleats, and soccer balls have to be dug out of wherever they were tossed last November, grass and mud dried between the cleats, the ball now a bit wilted. Or take a Thursday night in December, when you remember that your kindergartner's class is supposed to decorate two dozen gingerbread cookies the next day. Where did you put that king-size jar of ground ginger that you bought last

month? On the pantry shelf next to the baking powder? In the cupboard next to the flour canister? Maybe it's still in the crate with the 1,000 cups, plates, and napkins bought at the same big-box store. Where is that crate?

While we all know that life would be much more pleasant if we were all perfectly organized, trying to get to that point can feel like a monumental

task. I hope that *Taunton's Home Storage Idea Book* will help demystify the process of designing good storage and help you use the resources available to create household storage that is both attractive and functional.

Approaching storage design systematically will help you tackle this big project, while also helping to ensure that the proper storage system is chosen. *Taunton's Home Storage Idea Book* moves through the major areas of a house with specific storage ideas and examples for each room. Keep in mind that this book shows storage in real, lived-in houses, with no product photos interspersed. You can learn a tremendous amount from studying catalogs and stores that sell storage products, and these products will solve many of your storage dilemmas. However, seemingly good storage concepts don't always translate to real-world functionality, so I've chosen to examine storage that works in its natural environment.

But before you begin, you must first rid yourself of what you don't really need or love. Life hasn't changed much since the 19th century, when Thoreau suggested that we "simplify, simplify." Do try to simplify, first by getting rid of old things that no longer have a purpose—be it practical or sentimental—and then by forging ahead and devising storage for the objects that you're pretty sure you can't live without, plus some.

—Joanne Bouknight

1

The Ins and Outs of Organizing

Getting organized means different things to different people. For some, it's a call to pare down possessions and donate anything that's no longer needed to charity. For others, it means adding things like a sturdy set of shelves so that a collection of books has a permanent place to reside. Then there are those who are somewhere in between. They see the organizing process as both adding and subtracting—a chance to reduce and renew while making their home a more enjoyable place to live. For others still, organizing is a chance to rethink how they live, what they keep, and how they keep it.

But no matter what organizing means to you, chances are it has the same gratifying effect: It makes you feel good. Just think of the feeling of satisfaction that washes over you after you've accomplished even the smallest organizing feat, like cleaning out your purse or briefcase. Putting things in order has the uncanny ability to make us think a little clearer and breathe a little easier.

THE BIG PICTURE

Before you donate long-forgotten items to charity or buy a new chest of drawers to store out-of-season clothing or gear, stop for a moment. Step back and consider your

◄ A WELL-ORDERED HOME STARTS AT THE FRONT DOOR. Here, a sturdy bench provides a place to rest while putting on or taking off shoes; cubbies, one for each member of the family, organize coats, hats, and other outdoor gear.

► WIRE RACKS LIKE THE ONES shown here are one of the many tools available for maximizing shelf space and improving the functionality of your kitchen cabinets.

▼ AN ALTERNATIVE TO CLASSIC PEGBOARD, a tongue and groove panel system that accepts wire baskets and hooks is ideal for organizing tools and garden gear.

whole house, not just one room or area. By contemplating the bigger picture before adding or subtracting things, you can be assured that you won't later regret giving away those red corduroy pants that you never wear but still adore. You'll also save yourself from getting rid of seemingly useless items that, with a little creative thinking, can actually serve a useful purpose. For instance, those old metal bicycle baskets may appear as piles of junk in your garage, but clean them off and hang them on the bathroom wall and you've got yourself a few sturdy, albeit eclectic, baskets for storing toiletries, towels, even magazines.

ASSESS THE SITUATION

Assessing the larger situation at hand requires that you see your home—and all of its clutter—in a new way. To help you be objective, grab a pad of paper and a pen, and survey each room. Pretend you're a stranger and write down the things in each space that need improvement. Are there too many coats piled in the front foyer? Does the dining room table serve as a dumping ground for mail? Do you have to push a pile of clothes off the bed before you can climb into it at night? These are the types of questions you must ask yourself as you move from room to room.

Performing this often-overlooked step at the start will ensure that you create an organizing plan that fits your lifestyle. For example, if mail does pile up on the dining room table and there's no way to get around that, perhaps you can outfit the table with an attractive basket that can corral the envelopes and magazines. Then when you want to use the room for dining, cleaning off the table is easy—simply remove the basket and the table is ready to be set. Or,

▲ IF THE ENTRANCE YOUR FAMILY USES every day opens into your kitchen, follow this homeowner's lead and convert a pair of base cabinets into locker-style cubbies for coats, bags, and other outdoor gear. Pull-out baskets, which would normally be used for storing vegetables, can accommodate hats, gloves, and scarves.

▲ **CABINETS ARE ESSENTIAL** organizing tools. Here, they help maintain order in this utility room, offering open shoe cubbies and closed-door types for supplies; a message board makes it easy to track when supplies are running low.

if clothes tend to get heaped on your bed, perhaps installing pegs or hooks on the bedroom wall or on the back of the closet door will provide additional space for your wardrobe. The important thing to remember is that getting organized isn't about changing the way you live, but rather it's about accommodating your lifestyle.

If you're still unsure about why you should create lasting order in your home, consider the person who decides to clean his closet. Before he makes a full assessment of his wardrobe, he typically rushes to the

store and stocks up on hangers, shoe boxes, garment bags, and other organizational gear. Three months later, the closet is in complete disarray again. Why? Because he never took the time to fully evaluate the situation and consequently stocked up on storage supplies that, in the end, only added to the mess. Sure, the right gear is important, but perhaps every article of clothing doesn't belong on a hanger. Perhaps shirts should be hanging and pants would be better kept folded on shelves. Bottom line: Think before you buy. Don't stock up on organizing

▶ A CLOSET BECOMES INSTANTLY UNORGANIZED when hangers get jumbled together. Replace all wire hangers with plastic-coated types to keep clothes hung straight and separate.

▼ AN ADJUSTABLE SHELVING SYSTEM will improve the inner workings of any closet. In this kitchen space they help keep pans, canned goods, and other cooking gear in order.

▲ WHEN PLACED NEAR A STOVE or cooktop, a narrow pullout cabinet is the perfect place to stow spatulas, ladles, and other utensils, freeing valuable counter space.

▼ **PERFECT FOR SMALL SPACES,** a cabinet or armoire can be outfitted to accommodate an alternate use. Here, door-mounted baskets keep current projects close at hand, while magnetized containers keep essential supplies like paper clips and rubber bands tidy.

▶ **WHETHER YOU'RE STOWING** office supplies in your desk or socks in a dresser, the rule of thumb is to group like items in smaller containers. Here, a compartmentalized tray keeps desktop essentials orderly.

supplies without getting real about how you live or what you really need to keep.

PLAN YOUR ATTACK

Once you've completed your walk-through, establish a plan of attack. If you're the type who is easily distracted or has difficulty prioritizing, take a step back and give everything on your list a stress rating (a number from 1 to 10, with 10 being the most worrisome) that indicates the extent to which the problem in question bothers you. For example, if your kitchen scores a 10, then that's where you should focus your energy—the bedroom, bathroom, and garage will simply have to wait.

Start Small

Tackling the biggest project first may seem overwhelming, but don't let the process get the best of you. The key to organizing any space is simply getting started. And to do that, you need only take your first small step. So while all of the corners of your kitchen may be screaming for your attention, focus on one pint-sized area. Begin with the junk drawer, for example. After

◀ **LIMITING THE AMOUNT** of floor storage in a small bathroom will help the room feel larger and more tidy. If you go this route, be sure to use wall space wisely, enlisting the aid of multiple towel racks and shelving over the sink.

emptying the contents and discarding dried-out pens, dead batteries, expired coupons, and other things you no longer need, examine what remains. Group like items, then outfit the drawer with plastic, metal, or wire bins that are sized to fit what you have to store. The bins will not only help you maintain order, but they also will make it possible to find what you need fast. Or start even smaller: Free up precious drawer space by moving your table linens from a kitchen drawer to a basket that can be set on a shelf next to the dining room table. This will give you extra room for storing utensils or other cooking items and put napkins and table-cloths where you need them most.

Others problems, like establishing a place for everything in a kitchen that has only a handful of cupboards, will require more of an investment—both emotionally and monetarily. But once you begin to solve smaller organizing issues, you'll be ready to dive into these bigger challenges. If you simply can't pare down your china or cookware, for instance, you may have to augment the existing storage by adding a freestanding cupboard or island. If your counter is overrun with cookbooks, leaving you no place to work, you may need to clean out a cabinet or add a sturdy set of shelves. Don't forget: What matters is not how much you have left to do but that you're making progress!

RULES TO LIVE BY

Whether you're beginning your journey to a more organized way of living by tackling small spaces one at a time or reworking every room in your house at once, keep the following guidelines in mind:

► **WHAT'S THE SECRET** to getting kids to put away their belongings? Implement an easy-to-follow storage system and label everything with words and pictures. The bins that help keep this armoire tidy are painted with chalkboard paint and labeled with chalk so markings can be easily changed.

• **Storage and organizing go hand in hand.** What's more, good storage saves steps. Strive to stow things where they're used, and group them by task or activity. For example, the best place to keep soup ladles, spatulas, and other cooking utensils is near the stovetop. Also avoid forcing yourself to learn new habits. If shoes are always piling up by the door, create storage for them there by adding a large bin or basket.

• **The more often you use something, the more accessible it should be.** Items you use everyday, like car and house keys, should be at your fingertips. Items you use a couple of times a month, like files for sorting bills, should be fairly easy to reach. Things that are used once a year, like holiday decorations, are best kept in out-of-the-way places like garages, basements, or attics.

• **When packing things away, never underestimate the power of a good-looking label.** It can spare you the hassle of digging through unmarked boxes. More important, well-labeled shelves and containers help everyone in your household remember at a glance where things belong. Another idea: Photograph each container's contents and tape the image to the box. This visual inventory will make things less likely to go astray.

• **You don't have to spend a lot—or even any—money to get yourself more organized.** Instead, tap into your home's hidden poten-

tial. Empty existing closets of things you no longer use. Repeat the process with bookshelves and cabinets. The spare spaces you uncover may be all the room you need to get your home life in order.

• **Don't skimp.** While saving money is a good thing, make sure that the ways you go about cutting costs don't end up cramping your lifestyle. For example, if you love to cook but don't because your kitchen is a recipe for disaster, spend the money to make it better. Add extra shelves to cabinets, or even add extra cabinets, so you can easily find the things you need.

• **Understand that it's okay to ask for help.** If the thought of emptying your closets of their contents, sorting through everything, and placing it all back in an orderly fashion has your head spinning, know that there are professionals who can help by assessing your situation and devising a plan of attack. To find one in your area, contact the National

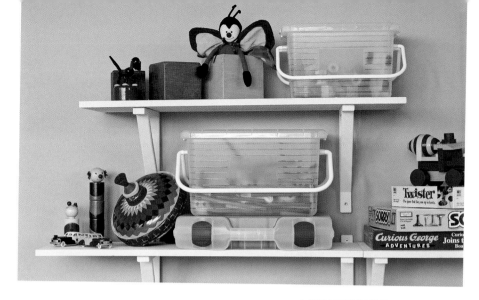

Association of Professional Organizers by logging on to www.napo.net, or look under Professional Organizers in the Yellow Pages of your local phone book.

▲ THE MORE OFTEN you use something, the more accessible it should be. Because the owner of this kitchen likes to entertain, platters, trays, and other serving items are kept in the open.

▲ YOU DON'T HAVE TO SPEND a lot of money to organize your child's belongings. Here, simple wood shelves get toys off the floor. Plastic bins with handles for easy toting hold playthings, like buildings blocks, that have multiple pieces.

KEEPING ORDER

While it's true that a well-organized home is easy to maintain, doing so requires that you do a little each day in order to stay on track. Spend 15 minutes going through the mail when you get home each night. And keep two piles, one for magazines and catalogs and another for bills and letters; go through the catalogs once a week and recycle what you don't want. You'll maintain order, too, if you put things away as soon as you're finished using them. For example, if you've finished with a library book, place it in a bag by your door rather than in a pile in the living room. This way, when you head out to work, you can grab the bag and return the book on your way home. Every month, tackle a particular room in your home. And twice a year, schedule a major cleaning.

Organizing is a skill, not a talent. With a little forethought and some effort on your part, you can regain control of your life—not to mention find those house keys you've misplaced once again.

2

Entryways

I f your home is like most, you probably have to step over a pile of coats and bags to get through the front door. It's a common problem of such high-traffic areas. However, with a little organization, it's possible to turn a clogged entry into space that says "welcome home" every time you pass through it. Plus, you want to greet visitors and guests with a good first impression, not a cluttered mess. Pretty is important, but practical is better.

With a little creative thinking, you can transform this space with furniture and accessories you already have. A chest of drawers, for example, can become a landing spot for car keys and the day's mail as well as storage for seasonal items such as hats and gloves. With the addition of a lower shelf, a bench not only becomes a place to take off shoes but also a place to stow them. If floor space is limited, take advantage of the surrounding walls. Peg boards and hooks require little room and can get most anything off the floor and out of the way. And whatever you do, don't forget the kids. If you want them to put away their belongings the moment they walk in the door, make sure it's convenient for them to do so.

◄ A STAIR TREAD EXTENDED around the corner of the staircase creates a handy built-in bench in this entry. Although it would have been easier and less expensive simply to add a seat, this clever design not only creates cohesiveness between two distinct spaces but also adds architectural interest.

Outerwear and Outdoor Gear

Whether your home's primary place of entry is a formal front hall or a casual mudroom, without the right organization plan, the space will become piled with coats, shoes, bags, and other daily essentials. Although corralling clutter behind a closet door is ideal, it's not always the most practical solution—especially when you factor in the number of times that you and your family pass through this space each day, needing the very things that are shut away. A better plan is to have organized storage out in the open where it is easily accessible morning through night. A custom built-in unit with hooks, pegs, and open shelves, for instance, will make reaching for a jacket on brisk mornings or cool evenings an effortless task.

▲ NO CLOSET REQUIRED. An alcove, like the one shown here, will easily organize gear. Simply outfit the space with hooks and shelves as you would a closet. To maximize the space, stack hooks vertically in rows; just be sure to measure first so the coats on the highest row don't cover those below.

◄ SEATING IS A USEFUL ADDITION to any foyer, providing a place to rest while lacing up boots and shoes. By adding a shelf below this built-in bench, the owners created two levels of storage, preventing footwear from piling up haphazardly on the floor.

◄ NO MUDROOM? No worries. An upholstered bench with built-in cubbies—and smaller matching wall unit—easily accommodates all types of indoor and outdoor gear. In lieu of traditional rubber boot trays, use metal cookie sheets to protect rugs or carpets from mud and moisture.

▼ EVEN THE SMALLEST OF SPACES, like the nook to the left of this door, can be made more efficient. All that's required are a few hooks and a bench that's sized to fit the space. Covering the floor with linoleum is ideal since it's easy to wipe up on wet days.

THE PROS KNOW

Transform your foyer into a more functional space with the following furnishings:

- A mirror lets you check your appearance before heading out the door.
- A bench provides a resting place while putting on or taking off shoes. Those with seats that lift up offer the added benefit of additional storage.
- An armoire stores out-of-season clothing and gear when closet space is limited.
- A chest or table serves as a temporary resting place for mail, packages, and keys.

Mudroom Basics

Converting a side or back entrance into a full-fledged mudroom will go a long way toward preventing pile-ups by your front door. Of course, the larger your entry, the more options you'll have, but even small spaces can contain a mudroom. Here's what to include:

- A closet, armoire, or built-in cabinet that can be used to store seasonal outerwear
- Baskets or bins for sports equipment
- Shelves to raise book bags, boxes, and other large items off the floor
- A bench or chair for changing shoes
- Bins for incoming and outgoing mail

- Hooks or containers for keys
- A stand for umbrellas
- Pegs or hooks for coats, jackets, and hats
- A resilient floor such as linoleum or vinyl that's easy to clean
- Waterproof containers for wet clothing

And if you have a pet, don't forget:

- Hooks for leashes
- A pet door
- Storage for food
- Space for a dog bed or sleeping quarters

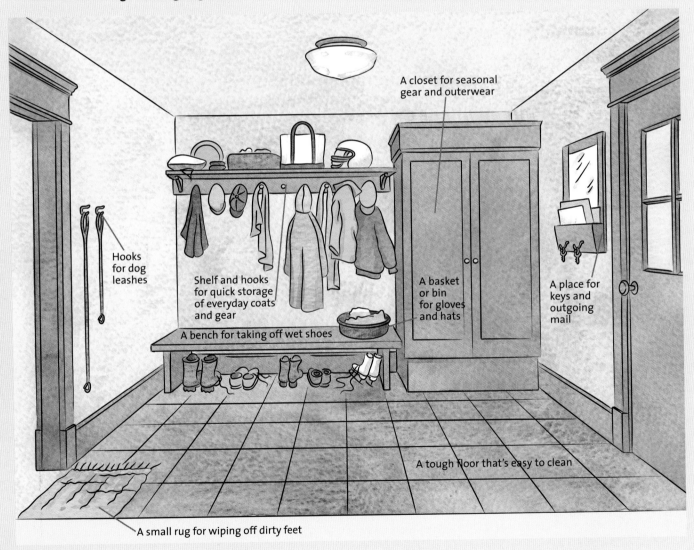

A closet for seasonal gear and outerwear

Hooks for dog leashes

Shelf and hooks for quick storage of everyday coats and gear

A bench for taking off wet shoes

A basket or bin for gloves and hats

A place for keys and outgoing mail

A tough floor that's easy to clean

A small rug for wiping off dirty feet

▲ AN ALTERNATIVE TO TRADITIONAL CLOSETS, locker-style built-ins have the added advantage of being open and easy to reach—a plus where kids are concerned. If space permits, provide one section for each member of your family.

▲ THIS NARROW MUDROOM is put to best use with a simple built-in with drawers. The same effect could be achieved with stacked storage cubes or ready-to-assemble cabinets.

◄ PEGS AND HOOKS are perhaps one of the easiest organizing tools available today. They make the most of this small apartment entryway.

A Foyer for All Seasons

Keep your front entry tidy by following these suggestions for handling the gear needed for different types of weather.

Cold Weather

- Keep only in-season coats, jackets, scarves, and hats in the closet or near the entryway door.

- If you're using hooks and pegs, designate one spot for each family member so that one person's items are all together.

- Keep hats and gloves in the sleeve of a coat to keep them from ending up on the floor (or on the wrong person!).

Warm Weather

- Replace the umbrella stand with a receptacle for sports equipment and other outdoor gear.
- Pack a bag for the beach or park and leave it in the hall closet.
- Hang bike helmets and baseball caps by the straps so they stay put.

Wet Weather

- Change a decorative doormat to a more rugged style that can easily handle heavy, messy boots.

- Leave a basket of old bath towels by the door in case a guest, family member, or pet needs to dry off when he comes inside.

- Set out a galvanized metal tray or several cookie sheets to collect wet boots and shoes.

▲ A ROW OF STURDY HOOKS and a simple bench ease the transition between indoors and out. A nearby walk-in closet with a wall of built-ins provides hidden but easily accessible storage for hats, gloves, and other gear.

▲ STORAGE DOESN'T HAVE TO STAND OUT. Instead, make it an extension of the architecture of the space. In this mudroom, the coat pegs, made from the same wood used to frame the door, blend into the room. A covered bench is a practical solution for hiding gear that's not in season.

◀ IF THE DOOR YOUR FAMILY REGULARLY USES leads from the driveway or garage to the kitchen, convert a pantry-style cabinet into open storage for outdoor items. After removing the doors, line the shelves with wicker baskets. Add a row of hooks for jackets, bike helmets, even cloth shopping bags.

◄ PRACTICAL CAN BE GOOD-LOOKING. Line the walls of your mudroom with open cubbies sized to fit all types of things you use when heading in or out the door. Hooks make it easy to put coats and umbrellas away quickly while benches provide ample space to spread out. A stone floor is a practical choice for easy cleanup.

Be Creative with the Ordinary

Sometimes the best storage solutions are right under your nose. For example, this laundry sorter embellished with appliquéd sports balls finds new purpose as an organizer for everything from hockey sticks to footballs. Other everyday items can assist you in your organizing efforts. Here are a few useful ideas:

- Hang a canvas shoe organizer on the back of a closet door and use the pockets to store hats and gloves during the winter.
- Stash summer gear in mesh laundry bags. This way, you won't have to hunt for towels, toys, or sunscreen when it's time to head to the beach. Instead, you can simply grab your bag and go.
- Use an accordion-style drying rack to keep scarves in order.

► FIND NEW USES FOR OLD EQUIPMENT. Here, a wheeled laundry sorter is used to corral sports gear. When not in use, simply roll the cart into a nearby closet.

Information Centers

AN ENTRY CAN BE MORE THAN A PLACE to welcome guests and collect coats. With the right storage pieces, it can also double as a message and mail-sorting center as well as a place to stockpile essential supplies like flashlights, batteries, and spare keys. An appropriately sized chest or console, for example, can serve all of these functions. Or you can forgo furniture altogether. The area beneath a staircase or an empty wall adjacent to the front door can be converted to usable storage with the addition of shelves or built-ins. Even the back of a closet door can be transformed into practical space: Adding a bulletin board or chalkboard makes it a family message center.

▲ WHAT'S THE EASIEST WAY to create a family message center? Mount a chalk or dry erase board over the place where everyone keeps their coats.

▲ A MESSAGE CENTER can be as simple as a wall-hung basket. Here, the basket is hanging from a coat rack, doubling the usefulness of this narrow entrance.

◄ A HALL TABLE provides plenty of surface area for setting mail and packages, but a cabinet with doors and drawers can be more practical—especially if you outfit the drawers with store-bought bins. Sized to hold keys, tape, and other small items, bins will keep clutter off the table top.

▲ THIS KITCHEN DRAWER was mounted on full-extension drawer slides, so reaching all the plastic containers of essential supplies is easy and allows the drawer to function as a family command center.

Creating a Command Center

Whether you're married or single, live in small or large space, every household requires a specific place for handling all the paper and information related to daily life—things like schedules for school activities, invitations to parties, reminders for doctors' appointments, bills, and other necessary notices. And according to organizing experts, the best place for this command center is near an exterior door that everyone in the family must enter or exit at some point during the day. The easiest solution: a wall-mounted bulletin board with pockets for mail, messages, and writing supplies. Of course the center need not be the first thing you see when you walk in the door. For example, if you opt to use the front hall, consider hanging a notice board and a large envelope, basket, or folder for each family member on the back of a closet door or inside an armoire. While the message center will be out of sight to visiting guests, it won't be out of mind to family members who will have to go into the closet to put away outdoor gear.

► TO MAKE SURE YOUR FAMILY sees important notices, place your message center in close proximity to where they hang their coats when they come in the door. These cubbies were designed with a bulletin board on one end to accommodate invitations, shopping lists and other important notes.

Kitchens

I n most homes, the kitchen is the hub—the one room where friends and family gather regularly to prepare meals, exchange stories, and catch up on the day's events. So why not make it an efficient workspace and an inviting place to hang out? Don't feel limited by the existing storage. And don't feel as though you need to do a full-blown remodel to make the space more functional. With a little ingenuity and a few store-bought accessories, you can efficiently tackle the pile of plates in your cupboards and the stacks of cookbooks that line your counters. You can deal with all of the plastic containers you've collected but never used, and finally make sense of that junk drawer. With a little forethought, pots and pans can be consolidated on a single rack near the stove, and linens and utensils can be corralled in baskets that are kept near the kitchen table. The goal is to arrange everything in a commonsense fashion so the heart of your home is both an easy place to use and an enjoyable place to gather.

◄ THE POTS IN THIS KITCHEN are contained on a rod that's recessed inside the framework of the cabinetry that surrounds the range. A plate rail is used to organize lids on the wall behind the pots, while cooking utensils are conveniently hung beneath the range hood.

Essential Ingredients

ECAUSE FOOD PREPARATION is a kitchen's primary purpose, there should be plenty of places for storing nonperishable items. How and where you do this depends both on how your kitchen is arranged and the quantity of supplies that you want to keep on hand. For example, if you shop once a month and buy in bulk, you'll probably find a walk-in pantry with generous shelf space most useful. If you shop at least once a week, however, you may be able to get by with several shelves in a single cabinet. In either case, the key to storing ingredients is having every item in view and within reach.

▲ TO MAKE IT EASIER to keep tabs on how much sugar, spice, or other dry goods remain in your pantry, remove these items from their packaging and store them in glass jars. Lining the jars on open shelves makes finding what you need a snap—especially when you're in a hurry.

◄ IF YOUR KITCHEN HAS AN ISLAND, make sure you're using it to it's best potential. Relegate cooking or serving gear there, to better the flow around the appliances.

◄ IF YOU BUY IN BULK and have run out of places to stash your savings, convert a closet near your kitchen into a small walk-in pantry. Install adjustable shelves and add a notice board to the back of the door so you can note when supplies are running low.

QUICK FIX

Counter Cures

Clear the clutter on kitchen countertops in five simple steps.

- Stash take-out menus in an expandable file folder. Sort the menus by cuisine, and place the file in a cabinet or drawer near the phone.
- If reading the paper is part of your morning ritual, place a basket near the breakfast table and toss the paper in it when you are done. Recycle when the basket is full.
- Transfer flour, sugar, rice, and other staples from bags to large, clear canisters or jars with airtight lids. Store those you use daily on your counter, and place the remainder in your pantry.
- Group whisks, spatulas, ladles, and other cooking utensils in vases, pitchers, or canisters.
- Dump your big, bulky appliances in favor of smaller versions that can easily mount underneath overhead cabinets.

▲ LOCATED BELOW THE MICROWAVE, this extra-deep base cabinet is outfitted with pullout pantry shelves and stocked with snacks. Because it's outside the kitchen's main cooking zone, kids can grab items for after-school snacks without getting in the way of dinner preparations.

FOODSTUFFS

▲ IF KITCHEN SPACE IS AT A PREMIUM, install a shelf about 12 in. from the ceiling. Use it to store items like rice and pasta that you don't need everyday. So you're able to see what's on hand without climbing a ladder, keep items in glass jars.

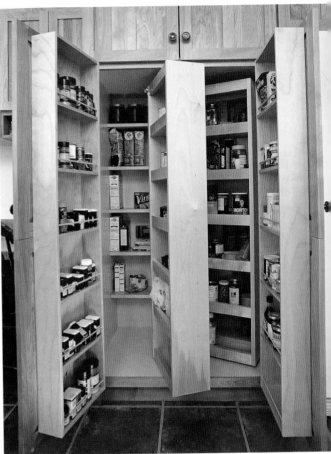

▲ SO THAT YOU DON'T HAVE TO HUNT all over your kitchen for essential ingredients every time you want to bake a batch of cookies, keep all of your non-perishable supplies in one central place, like a large pantry cabinet with multiple layers of shelves.

▲ BY ADDING RESTAURANT-GRADE metal shelves on either side of this freestanding range, the owners of this kitchen made it possible to keep cookbooks and cooking gear where they're needed. Topping the shelves with butcher block, which can function as a cutting board, adds to their usefulness.

◄ CONSIDER STORING STAPLES like flour, rice, and coffee in a base cabinet with glide-out drawers. Because the shelves pull toward you, you'll have an easy time finding what you need, even if it's stowed way in the back. Drawers with high sides ensure that items stay securely in place as the unit glides back and forth.

▲ AN ODD ALCOVE left over from an earlier remodeling becomes a useful walk-in pantry in this kitchen. When organizing a space such as this, remember that shelving doesn't have to stop at your height; it can go all the way up to the ceiling and be used for stashing items that are reserved for special occasions.

▼ IF YOU'RE SHORT ON STORAGE, think outside the box. Additional "pantry" space was added to this kitchen by lining one wall of the adjoining service staircase with floor-to-ceiling shelves that are deep enough to hold one bottle, can, or jar. Added bonus: This type of storage is also ideal for displaying decorative items like plates and platters.

◄ WHETHER YOU CHOOSE built-in or freestanding cabinets, outfitting an otherwise unused wall in a kitchen with floor-to-ceiling storage is always a wise investment since you can never have too many places to put things.

▼ TO FREE COUNTER SPACE for small appliances that you use on a regular basis, mount a shallow shelf in the open space between the bottom of the cupboard and the top of the counter. Use the shelf to store jars of baking ingredients, canisters, and other items that would otherwise clutter the counter.

Wine Storage Made Simple

It's fine to store everyday wine in the kitchen, but if you have an extensive collection—or exceptional bottles—a cool (50°F to 60°F), dry place, like a basement, is essential. And because wine should be stored on its side to prevent the cork from drying out and the wine from spoiling, you'll need bins or racks with angled shelves to hold the bottles in place. If a full-fledged wine cellar isn't an option, consider a wine refrigerator. Available in sizes that hold anywhere from 24 to more than 100 bottles, these specialized cooling centers can be installed under counters or islands or in a run of cabinets, just like a standard refrigerator or freezer.

▶ INSTALL WINE RACK DRAWER SLIDES to an existing base cabinet to make wine storage—and retrieval—simple.

SPICES

◀ THE EASIEST WAY to organize spices is by type of cuisine. Simply create a tray (an aluminum baking dish will work well) for Mexican or Indian dishes, for example, and fill several small containers with the essential spices. Label the tray as well as the individual containers so anyone can easily find what they need.

▲ THIS NARROW PULLOUT, which can be accessed from both sides, puts spices within close proximity to the cooktop, the area where they're used most. To cut down on prep time, store spices with those used most often on the top rack.

◀ FOR A LARGE COLLECTION OF SPICES, utilize a cabinet that can do double duty with a rack on the inside and one that's mounted on the back of the door. Place spices that are used every day on the door rack so they'll be in full view when you open the cabinet.

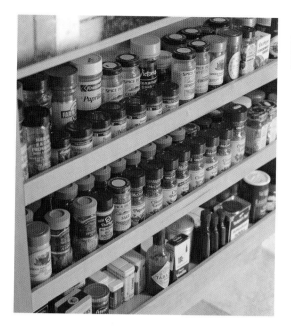

THE PROS KNOW

Store herbs and spices away from heat and light to preserve freshness and flavor. Replace them after six months because most herbs, by that time, have lost their potency.

◄ SMALL SHELVES WITH LIPS make organizing and identifying spices easy since the lips hold the bottles in place and you can easily see the label on each jar. Arrange the containers alphabetically to quickly find the spice your recipe calls for.

▲ CLUTTER ON THE COUNTERTOP is kept to a minimum in this sleek kitchen, where the spice rack is suspended over the cooktop from a stainless-steel rod. While this placement is fine for small amounts of frequently used spices, bulk storage should be located elsewhere, preferably in a cool, dry place.

Cooking Tools

GOOD FOOD CAN BE MADE FAST. The secret: efficient storage that puts all of your tools at your fingertips. The most obvious examples are metal racks for hanging pots and pans near a stove or cooktop. Other ideas include cabinets outfitted with vertical dividers to keep cookie sheets, cake pans, and baking items in good order, and canisters used to keep spoons, spatulas, and other utensils within easy reach. Even hanging a magnetic strip near your prep area for organizing knives will make slicing and dicing an effortless task. All of these ideas are simply starting points, however. By organizing the interiors of your cabinets, drawers, and pantry to suit your cooking style, you soon will have a kitchen that runs like a well-oiled machine.

▲ A POT RACK DOESN'T HAVE TO BE made of metal. It can also be crafted from wood, like this one, in a design that mimics your cabinets. The shelf above accommodates lids and pots that are too large to hang.

▲ MAKE A DEEP DRAWER more useful by organizing it with your collection of baking sheets and muffin trays stored vertically rather than horizontally in a stack. This will make it easier to find what you need.

▲ UNLESS YOU HAVE THE RIGHT ARRANGEMENT, storing pots and pans in cabinets can be a chore. Here, sliding bins keep cookware contained while offering simple access. To make it easy to find what you need, sort items by use. For example, keep your baking pans in one bin and your pots in another.

▲ POT RACKS ARE A PERFECT SOLUTION for serious cooks because they place cookware where it can be easily reached. To keep racks from becoming a jumbled mess, sort pots and pans by size, hanging the smallest in front and the largest in back.

The Inside Story on Storage

If your kitchen cabinets are bursting at the seams, sort through the contents and toss items you no longer need. Disposing of mismatched glasses, stacks of plastic containers, and broken appliances will free up valuable space and so will the following tasks:

- **Create deep storage.** Stash items that are used infrequently (think bread machines, food processors, and good china) on shelves in the garage, basement, or attic. Tape a running list of their locations inside one of your cabinets so you know where to find them when necessary.

- **Annex a wall.** Mount a sheet of pegboard or a metal rack on a wall near the range. Then, using hooks, hang your pots and pans.

- **Maximize shelf space.** Install hooks for hanging mugs and teacups. Add a wire rack to break up dishes into more manageable stacks.

- **Divide and conquer.** Retrofit a cabinet with a store-bought vertical racking system. Use it to keep unwieldy items like platters, baking sheets, and serving trays in order.

- **Retrofit existing cabinets.** Replace the shelves in base cabinets with full-extension pullout racks. This will make it easier to access formerly out-of-reach items.

POTS AND PANS

▲ TO KEEP YOUR DRAWER of plastic storage containers in good order, store them with lids intact. While this takes up a little more space, it saves time from hunting through a jumbled mess of mismatched tops and bottoms.

▼ KEEP ALL OF YOUR BAKING EQUIPMENT in one cupboard. To prevent the collection of trays, racks, and muffin tins from becoming a jumbled mess, outfit the cabinet with vertical dividers that will hold the pans upright.

▲ NO MATTER HOW LARGE YOUR KITCHEN, storing roasters and other oversized pans can be difficult especially since they rarely fit in standard size cabinets. Here, in this rustic kitchen, the pans are kept on a ceiling-mounted shelf out of the way, but within close reach.

THE PROS KNOW

The best way to ensure that your kitchen operates efficiently is to store items close to where you'll be using them. For example, hang pots and pans on a rack near the stove. Stash knives and cutting boards in a drawer near a prep sink. Store dinnerware close to the table or in close proximity to the dishwasher so cleanup is less of a chore.

Handy Uses for Hooks

- Hang dish towels to dry on the side of an island.
- Mount a rolling pin on a wall over a baking center.
- Attach pots and pans to a rack near the cooktop.
- Store mugs near the coffee maker.
- Hold wire baskets for keeping small items, like garlic and lemons, at the ready.

◄ WITH THE ADDITION of a wire grid, a common item at most home centers, an empty wall becomes easy-to-reach storage for pots, pans, and other cooking gear. Metal hooks hold the items in place.

▲ THE SMARTEST WAY TO ORGANIZE your kitchen is to place things at their point of use. Here, pots and pans are stored over the stove on hooks that attach to a metal rod, while cookbooks are kept on shelves beneath the island's prep surface.

COOKBOOKS

▲ IF YOU PREFER a clutter-free kitchen but your cookbook collection is extensive, consider stowing the volumes out of sight in deep drawers designed to hold pots or in cabinets with slide-out shelves. These custom cabinets slide out from the wall.

▲ KEEP ALL OF YOUR RECIPES in one place by storing cookbooks together on a dedicated set of shelves. When determining where to place them in your kitchen, look for a space that's within close proximity to the stove but also adjacent to ample counter space so there's room to spread out and work.

▲ STORING COOKBOOKS ON SHELVES that are part of a centrally located kitchen island makes them easily accessible from all points in the kitchen. Arranging the books by cuisine makes it easy to find a particular recipe.

▲ TO HELP CREATE a display shelf for cookbooks, the homeowners simply removed the doors from a set of cabinets, creating a cookbook niche.

► BY INCORPORATING SHELVING FOR COOKBOOKS above this desk, a kitchen niche becomes a dedicated space for planning family dinners. If you have a similar spot in your kitchen but cabinet doors cover the shelves, remove the doors to make it easier to access your family's favorite recipes.

THE PROS KNOW

Place recipes clipped from newspapers and magazines in plastic sleeves, and then store the sleeves in a three-ring binder. To help make finding a recipe easier, sort them by cuisine, occasion, prep time, or some other significant designator.

Dishware

A WELL-ORGANIZED KITCHEN will make cooking less of a chore; it will also simplify the serving process. To put your dishes, utensils, and linens in order, start by taking inventory of what you own, dividing the items into groupings based on how they are used. Everyday dinnerware is best kept on open shelves or in cabinets that are in close proximity to where you eat breakfast, lunch, and dinner. Seldom-used items, like Grandma's holiday china, are better stored in a secure location away from the bustling workspace such as the basement or attic. Padded containers will protect fine dinnerware from dust and damage.

▼ IF YOUR EVERYDAY DISHES don't stay organized behind closed doors, then try this stylish yet practical makeover: Store them in open shelves so that you know exactly where to turn when you need a specific item. If you have more than one set of dishes, stow plates, bowls, and cups according to color and size.

▲ CABINETS WITH BUILT-IN DISH DIVIDERS make it easy to retrieve dinnerware without pulling out an entire stack of dishes.

▼ DO YOU PREFER TO STORE your china behind closed doors? Then consider cabinets with shallow pullout shelves for convenient access. To make it easy to find what you need, store only like items on a shelf. For example, organize all of your covered serving dishes in one area and serving bowls in another.

▲ WIRE SHELVES ARE A SIMPLE SOLUTION for small budgets. What's more, they're easy to install and can be mounted anywhere—even over the range or cooktop, where they can be used to warm plates before serving.

Shelving Solutions

Increase the storage capacity of cabinets with the following store-bought accessories:

- **Plate racks.** Those with vertical slots prevent plates from rubbing against one another and chipping.
- **Shelf maximizers.** These wire racks with legs add a second layer to an ordinary shelf, allowing you to condense dishware into a smaller space by stacking cups and saucers over plates and bowls.
- **Pullouts.** Because these wire or plastic baskets slide out, you'll be able to reach items in the back with ease.
- **Tiered racks.** These stair-stepped shelves let you see with ease everything you've stored.
- **Cabinet door racks.** These devices convert the inside of cabinet doors into convenient storage spaces for foils and plastic wraps, even pot lids.

▼ DON'T WORRY if your cabinets can't accommodate oversized bowls, baskets, and serving platters. Take a cue from this kitchen by stacking them on an open baker's rack or even on a bookshelf.

▲ A WALL-MOUNTED DRYING RACK adds vintage charm to this classic kitchen while serving as a storage spot for dinnerware. Because the rack is mounted directly over the sink where dishes are washed, it makes cleanup easy. To glean extra storage for cleaning supplies, the homeowner curtained the area below the sink.

◄ BECAUSE THE OWNERS OF THIS KITCHEN eat most of their meals at the room's central island, they opted for a design with open shelving on one side so everyday dinnerware is kept close at hand. Added bonus: Because the shelves are shallow, things aren't likely to end up lost in the back.

▲ THERE'S NO REASON WHY your dishes should be hidden away in cabinets. Instead, use them to enhance your room's décor. Here, pastel-colored china adds a splash of color to this all-white kitchen.

Storage for Safekeeping

H ere's how to store fine flat-ware, china, and linens so that they're ready to use when you need them.

- Keep silver and silver-plated flat-ware in trays lined with velvet, felt, or another soft fabric to prevent scratches.
- Store platters, candlesticks, and other large silver pieces in fabric bags. If you place more than one item in a bag, place a piece of felt between each one.
- Set wine glasses and other delicate crystal mouth up to avoid damage.
- Place good china and glassware in quilted containers to protect pieces from dust and help prevent chipping and cracking.
- Reduce wrinkles by rolling fine linens in acid-free tissue around a cardboard tube. Store the tube in a drawer until needed.

▲ TO CONVERT THIS KITCHEN CLOSET into stylish storage, the owners replaced its standard wood doors with a more charming French pair and added wood paneling to the interior walls. The closet's extra-deep shelves afford plenty of room for keeping everyday dishes up front where they're easy to reach and seldom-used items in the back.

▼ THE CEILING-MOUNTED SHELF over this kitchen countertop is open on both sides so that dishes can be readily accessed from the dining and serving areas. Dividing the shelf into several smaller compartments simplifies the process of sorting glasses, cups, plates, and bowls.

▼ IF YOU HAVE AN EXTENSIVE COLLECTION of dinnerware, borrow an idea from the past—group your dishes by pattern, then stow them in glass-fronted cabinets. The glass doors serve a dual purpose: They make it simple to locate a particular design, and they keep the dishes dust free.

▲ ERGONOMIC ALTERNATIVES to traditional cabinets, drawers keep dishes at waist level, eliminating heavy overhead lifting. Wooden pegs, which can easily be reconfigured depending on what's stored, prevent dishes from sliding when the drawer is opened or closed.

▲ OPEN STORAGE allows for quick and easy access to dishes at a moment's notice. But it looks messy if not kept in some sense of order. Although it's ideal to keep like items together, you can mix things up provided the items share a common thread, like color or theme.

◄ IF YOU LACK DRAWER SPACE or want easy access to utensils while cooking, use simple ceramic or glass jars to keep wooden spoons, forks, and spatulas organized on your counter.

▼ RATHER THAN STOW EVERYDAY LINENS in drawers, which can be difficult to close when they're too full, stack them in baskets. The slide-out variety shown here is only available with cabinets made specifically for them, but you can create a similar scenario by simply stacking baskets on open shelves.

▲ SHALLOW DRAWERS with fitted dividers are essential for sorting silverware. Thanks to a double-tray design, this drawer can accommodate two sets. Although custom dividers are ideal, alternatives, such as wire or plastic containers, can be found at most home stores.

◄ WHILE DRAWER DIVIDERS ARE ESSENTIAL for sorting cutlery, those that can be removed make setting the table a snap since they allow knives, forks, and spoons to be carried to the table with ease.

Clean Sweep

What's the secret to a clean kitchen? Turns out it's keeping the area surrounding the sink clean. Here are a few ideas for keeping this often busy area tidy:

- Annex empty space, like the area immediately under the front of your sink. Install a narrow tilt-out drawer, and use it to hide sponges, scrub brushes, and scouring pads.
- Group garbage and recycling containers on a slide-out rack beneath the sink or island. Place several garbage bags in the bottom of each can so a new bag will be ready when a full one is removed.
- Store cleaning solutions and dishwashing detergents in pullout baskets or bins under the sink.
- If space permits, add a plate rack over the sink. Dishes are easiest to handle if stored between waist and chest height near where they are cleaned.

▲ A CENTRALLY LOCATED SET of recycling bins makes cleanup simple. For easier access, mount the containers on glide-out racks and conceal them behind cabinet doors.

◄ OUTFITTED WITH A GALVANIZED METAL TRAY, this tilt-out drawer, which can be retrofitted to existing cabinetry, turns what would otherwise be wasted space into a handy place for stashing sponges and scouring brushes. When closed, the tray's façade matches the style of the surrounding cabinets.

4

Gathering Places

Aside from your kitchen, what's the one room in your house that receives heavy use on a daily basis? More than likely it's the den or the living room—the space that holds the TV and all of your other media equipment, books, toys, and games. And whether this room is furnished formally with fine upholstered furniture or is more casual with a pair of slipcovered sofas, chances are it collects clutter. Why? Because trying to find places to stow all the stuff that make this room a great place to hang out in can be a challenge.

In addition to the usual media equipment (TV, DVD player, and stereo), there are bound to be stacks of books and magazines. If you have children, there will inevitably be a pile of toys. The solution to creating order in this space isn't to do away with the various pieces of equipment and things that entertain us, but rather to find ways of making them disappear when they're not in use. A wall of simple store-bought shelves, for example, can help you convert stacks of reading material into a well-organized library. A more costly but stream-lined solution is to install built-in cabinets, which in addition to containing books can also be used to conceal media equipment behind closed doors. The bottom line to organizing this active room is to keep items out of sight but not out of mind.

◄ **WHEN PLANNING A WALL OF BUILT-INS,** think about how they'll fit in with the overall de-sign of your space. Here, tall, narrow cases were selected to complement the striped paint treat-ment used on the walls. Several drawers below a built-in bench provide extra storage.

Media Equipment

IN THE PAST, MOST LIVING ROOMS WERE DESIGNED so that the fireplace was the focal point of the space. Today, however, the fireplace has been replaced by the TV—a move that many decorators lament for the simple reason that a TV surrounded by all of its accompanying equipment (DVD player, speakers, and cable box) is anything but an attractive site. Built-ins, cubbies, or storage units can easily correct the problem, but the proper placement is essential. After all, you want the screen to be visible from any angle but positioned so that glare won't interfere with daytime viewing. You'll also want to make sure that the storage device you choose, be it an armoire or set of shelves, can accommodate media accessories such as DVDs, CDs, and videos. Finally, get a handle on all of your components' cords and cables by utilizing ties or flexible tubing devices. Doing so will eliminate a tangled mess of wires and create a truly well-organized—and visually appealing—media center.

▲ A TALL AND NARROW CLOSET is transformed into a multilevel media center with the simple addition of custom shelves. Before retrofitting a closet or recessed space, look for electrical outlets. If none exist, have an electrician install one prior to construction.

Custom built-ins may be a good way to create unobtrusive storage for large items like televisions and stereos, but don't overlook the rest of the room. It also helps to buy furniture that can do double duty—coffee tables with drawers and end tables with shelves—by providing auxiliary places to tuck things, like the TV remote or a pad of paper for jotting notes, that are used everyday.

▼ IF YOU WANT TO CONCEAL MEDIA EQUIPMENT but can't justify the expense of custom built-ins or a large armoire, borrow this clever idea by stacking your equipment on a sturdy set of unfinished shelves. Disguise the unit by covering the frame with standard tab-top curtain panels.

▲ MEDIA EQUIPMENT doesn't have to be kept in an armoire. Here, a set of three niches, the largest sized to hold a television, convert an empty wall into a contemporary media cabinet. When adopting a design solution such as this, be sure to have electrical outlets installed at the back of each niche.

◄ TODAY'S LARGE-SCREEN TVS can easily overwhelm a room—even one like this with generous proportions. To prevent that from happening, try to visually minimize its impact on the space, such as recessing it into the wall cavity as was done here. This also allowed space for shelves above it, for storing other media equipment.

Streamline Media Equipment

Organize your media equipment in a snap by following these five easy steps:

- Group all of your equipment in a single cabinet or built-in.
- Invest in a universal remote that will control all of your equipment.
- Recess speakers into walls and ceilings where they don't take up valuable floor or shelf space.
- Transfer old cassette and video tapes you wish to keep to narrower space-saving CDs or DVDs. Throw out the old cassettes and tapes.
- Eliminate unused components. For example, if you haven't taken your turntable for a spin in years, it's time to get rid of it.

▼ A GEOMETRIC-SHAPED RECESS with custom shelving and cabinetry turns what would otherwise have been a blank wall into a full-fledged media center. Slide-out wire bins to the left of the television provide plenty of easy-access storage for DVDs.

◀ IN THIS MODERN LIVING ROOM, all eyes are focused on the TV, a flat-screen style that's incorporated into a custom-made built-in. The surrounding shelves provide ample storage space for books as well as for displaying decorative items. Below, drawers and cabinets conceal additional media and electronic equipment.

▶ THE OWNERS OF THIS MUSIC COLLECTION chose to stash their CDs in cabinets fitted with shallow slide-out shelves—a storage solution that makes it simple to search for a particular CD since cases are kept on end with the album title clearly visible.

Caring for Electrical Cords

Finding a place to put your media equipment is easy. Deciding how to handle the cords and wires that accompany the television, cable box, stereo receiver, and other components can be slightly more complicated, especially if your electrical outlets aren't in an accessible location. Fortunately, there are a number of easy-to-implement solutions available, like Velcro® ties, plastic clips, flexible tubing, and labels, many of which can be found at your local hardware store or home center.

◀ BECAUSE MEDIA CENTERS ARE COMPRISED of two or more pieces of equipment, electrical cords often become tangled and difficult to manage. Flexible plastic tubing, available at home centers, allow you to gather and conceal several cords, streamlining the surrounding area in the process.

▶ WHEN MORE THAN ONE CORD plugs into a power strip, it can be difficult to determine which cord belongs to what component. To solve that problem, identify each piece of equipment on a file folder label and then wrap it around each cord.

◀ A STRATEGICALLY PLACED POWER STRIP can prevent overload at a wall outlet by eliminating the need for long extension cords. To keep the cord that connects the strip to your power outlet from becoming tangled, first wind it in an oval pattern, and cinch its middle with a Velcro band or twist-ties from loaves of bread.

► WHEN ORGANIZING CDS AND DVDS, borrow an idea from a library. Stow the media devices in shallow drawers and outfit the drawer fronts with handles that accommodate labels. This way you'll be able to see at a glance where things are kept.

▲ STORAGE UNITS SIZED TO THEIR CONTENTS help keep the items organized and can maximize the space. This cabinet does double duty, with the CD storage unit inset into the cabinet, allowing enough room for a door-mounted cassette holder.

▲ JUST BECAUSE YOUR DVDS AND DVD player are hidden behind a cabinet door doesn't mean they shouldn't be organized. Divide the cabinet into sections, with each sized to house a specific component of your entertainment system. Shallow drawers should also be added to accommodate CDs and DVDs.

Remote Solutions

Whether you operate your TV with one remote control and your DVD player with another or have one complex unit that controls all of your media and audio equipment, establishing a dedicated storage space for your components' remotes will save you from having to look under the couch and turn over seat cushions every time you want a little entertainment. Here are a few creative places to store your family's most coveted item:

• Hand-sewn pouches that overlap a chair or sofa arm.
• A lidded decorative box on a coffee or side table.
• A small leather tray that can rest on a table next to your favorite chair.
• Small basket or bottle caddies with handles.

▲ BOTH PRINT AND ELECTRONIC MEDIA can happily coexist. The secret: designing a set of shelves that can accommodate both. To do so, you'll need to know the measurements of both your television and your books. You'll also need to have the shelving unit designed to accommodate an electrical connection.

Books

BOOKS, UNLIKE MANY OF THE BELONGINGS that clutter our homes, have the ability to add warmth and personality to any room. To have the most impact, however, your personal reading material should be grouped as a collection in one space. To that end, begin by taking inventory of your library, noting not only the subject matter (fiction, gardening, and history, for example) but also the dimensions of the books in your possession. Taking inventory at the start will help you determine the type as well as the dimensions of the shelving system you require. If your collection is small and comprised only of a few paperback novels, for instance, a simple store-bought bookcase will most likely meet your needs. If, however, you're an avid reader with an extensive library covering multiple topics, you may want to invest in something more substantial, like a wall of built-ins that not only houses your collection but also shows it off.

▶ IF YOUR BUDGET CAN'T ACCOMMODATE BUILT-INS, take a cue from this room and devise a basic shelving system that fits the look of the space. Here, to complement the room's clean, modern design, the owners of this space devised a shelving system using simple pine planks artfully arranged in a grid pattern.

▼ ALTHOUGH FLOOR-TO-CEILING BOOKSHELVES are a nice feature, sometimes they can make a spare, modern space feel cluttered. One way to prevent that from happening is to install a pair of sliding doors in front of the shelves. Then, when not in use, the bookshelves simply disappear.

▲ INSTEAD OF SIMPLY stacking books on an otto-
man or coffee table, place them in tray. Not only is
the presentation neater, but the books are also less
likely to wind up on the floor.

THE PROS KNOW

To make finding specific book titles easier, organize your library by
subject, using bookends or other sturdy decorative objects to denote
where one section ends and another begins. If your collection is size-
able and requires additional shelving space, remove cookbooks and
store them on a shelf or in a cabinet in the kitchen.

▲ WHEN ADDING BOOKCASES to a room, don't
necessarily go for the wall with the most open
surface area. Instead, look for smaller spaces that
would otherwise be left unused. Here, they were
added to a half wall that hides a staircase,
further delineating the separation of space.

THE PROS KNOW

► THE BEAUTY OF BOOKCASES is that they can go just about anywhere. Here, thanks to the addition of simple open shelving, an otherwise useless alcove becomes a cozy reading nook.

▼ INSTEAD OF LINING AN EMPTY WALL with floor-to-ceiling shelves, the owners of this space chose to place their units on either side of a doorway. The resulting symmetry not only makes for a more interesting entrance, but it also creates balance in the space.

Designing Shelves

While it's important that a bookcase fit the dimensions of the room in which you place it, it's equally important that it accommodate your collection of books. Here's how to find a set of shelves that will do both:

- To determine the number of shelves you need, measure the linear footage of the books, CDs, and other items you intend to store. For example, a shelf measuring 6 ft. in length offers 6 lin. ft. of storage.
- Measure the area of the room where the shelves will go.
- When commissioning a custom bookshelf, request that the depth of the shelf be 12 in. This will allow you to store most any size book with ease.
- Consider the weight of your collection. To ensure adequate support, shelves should be constructed out of wood that is no less than $3/4$ in. thick.
- For added support, place shelf supports every 30 in. If this is not possible because of space limits, restrict shelf length to no more than 30 in.
- Always leave room for extra shelves so your collection can expand.

▲ WITH FLOOR SPACE FILLED TO CAPACITY, the owners of this modern apartment took advantage of the double-height ceiling, using the extra wall space to install shelving units for books and display items around the perimeter of the room.

▶ STORAGE, ESPECIALLY FOR THINGS LIKE BOOKS, doesn't have to be confined to an actual room. Here, built-in shelving is used to give a hallway leading into a living room a second purpose.

Book Basics

If you want to make books last, dust them periodically using a vacuum with a brush attachment. Here are a few other important tips for maintaining your collection:

- Loosely pack hardcover books on shelves—with large books stored flat to avoid bending their spines—and arrange according to subject. Use bookends for even support, and leave dust jackets in place to protect covers.
- Line up small paperbacks vertically. Stack oversized paperbacks to avoid warping their spines.
- Keep books with leather covers at moderate temperature and humidity levels. Heat and dryness can crack tanned leather, and dampness can cause swelling.

▲ STANDARD SIZE BOOKCASES are great, but for a truly custom fit you need a built-in, like this unit, which acts as both book storage and room divider. It provides the perfect backdrop for the sofa, and allows for easy removal and storage of books.

▲ IF YOUR READING COLLECTION is small and space is at a premium, consider a coffee table with shelves that can accommodate several stacks of books.

◄ THIS SPACE IS WELL ORGANIZED and tidy even though it's filled with lots of furniture. The sofa table acts as a backup to the bookshelf for book storage.

▲ THE CUSTOMIZED SHELVING in this living room is shallow but holds quite a few books and accessories due to the use of adjustable shelves, which allow for maximum flexibility.

5

Private Spaces

Let's face it: Life is complicated, and it's not always possible to leave the pressures of the world around us outside the home. That's why within every home there needs to be an escape—a private place where we can relax and unwind when the day is done. In most homes, this responsibility falls on the master suite, the one area of the house that's already off limits to everyone but immediate family. But relaxing, even in rooms that are designed specifically for this purpose, can be difficult, especially when the floor is covered with clothes that haven't been put away or the bathroom counter is clogged with so many toiletries that it looks like a shelf at your local drugstore. The solution: Find a convenient place for everything by purging your belongings and reworking or adding to your existing storage. Start small. Clean off a shelf in your linen closet so there's a place to store excess grooming products. Then assess your furnishings. Would replacing a small bedside table with a chest of drawers help your organizing issues? Finally, take an inventory of your wardrobe. If you haven't worn an item in more than a year, get rid of it and free up some valuable closet space. After all, less really is more.

◄ WHEN IT COMES TO MAXIMIZING STORAGE in the bedroom, don't overlook the space under the bed or surrounding it. Just as nightstands work wonders for keeping reading materials close at hand, a chest at the foot of the bed provides easy-access storage for spare blankets and pillows.

Bedrooms

BEDROOMS, NO MATTER THEIR SIZE, never seem to have enough storage. As a result, clothes pile up at the foot of the bed and the night table becomes buried in a stack of books. The result is a retreat that's anything but restful. To remedy the situation, take stock of what you store in the space. For example, do you really need those plaid pants you haven't worn in five years? Once you weed out the things that are no longer necessary, you'll find that it's much easier to organize the room. If, for instance, you are an avid reader, you may want to consider a headboard that incorporates shelving. If the culprit is an excess of clothing, you may to need to invest in a larger chest of drawers or a set of shallow storage boxes that can slide neatly under your bed. What you'll discover as you assess the contents of the room is that with a little planning it's quite possible to create a space where everything has its place.

▲ LOOKING FOR AN EASY WAY to keep clothes from piling up on the bedroom floor? Install racks of pegs or hooks around the perimeter of your room. You'll find them useful for holding everything from bathrobes and belts to purses and pants.

◄ ONE OF THE BENEFITS OF BUILT-INS is that they can make an otherwise useless space, like the area between the bed and a wall, useful. The unit here, a sort of sideboard that butts up to the edge of the bed, features shelves that are deep enough to accommodate various night-table necessities.

THE PROS KNOW

When space is tight, purchase low-profile storage boxes and bins. Fill them with out-of-season clothing and stash the items under the bed.

▲ IF YOU'RE AN AVID NIGHTTIME READER but your bedside table is too small to cope with a large stack of books, add a set of recessed shelves over the bed. If you don't feel like knocking into a wall or if built-ins aren't in your budget, opt for a simple store-bought unit.

Create a Restful Retreat

Here's how to make sure that clutter isn't the last thing you see when you go to bed at night or the first thing you see when you wake up in the morning.

- Outfit the top drawer in your dresser or bedside table with small plastic containers, shallow boxes, or baskets in which to store bedroom supplies and accessories like watches and rings.
- Fit the backs of closet doors with hooks that can be used to hold accessories that tend to pile up on chairs and benches.
- Move your current reading material off your nightstand, and store it on a nearby shelf or in a basket under the bed.

▲ THIS SLEEPING SPOT OWES its spare appearance to a wall of built-in cupboards opposite the foot of the bed. To keep the drawers from becoming a mess, identify one for each type of clothing, like socks and undergarments, shirts, sweaters, and anything else that needs to be folded.

To prevent dirty clothes from piling up on the bedroom floor, outfit your closet with hampers or laundry bags for colored, white, and dry-clean-only wash. Then, when you get undressed, place what you've worn in the appropriate bag and your clothes will be ready for the laundry.

▼ SOMETIMES THE SIMPLEST IDEAS are the best. Here, a recessed shelf replaces the headboard, providing a place to stash reading materials, glasses, and a host of other necessities that may be needed in the middle of the night.

The Nature of Nightstands

When it comes to choosing bedside storage, forgo the expected matching nightstands in favor of a mixed set that fits your needs as well as your partner's. Here's what to consider:

- Bedside tables that include shelves are ideal for those who not only like to read in bed but also like to keep a stack of books on hand at all times.

- A chest of drawers is a wise choice if you have supplies for a hobby, such as knitting, that you like to work on in bed before retiring for the night.

- Some pieces of furniture can perform more than one function. When not holding a stack of books, a sturdy hall chair can provide a comfortable place to sit while putting on shoes.

- A small, round table fits the bill if you have nothing to stash, save for an alarm clock and a lamp.

▲ THE ADJUSTABLE SHELVES that frame the window in this guest bedroom turn otherwise wasted space into practical storage for books and other treasures. The daybed is another practical space saver because it can be used for an overnight guest or as a quiet place to read.

▲ LOW-PROFILE BUILT-IN SHELVES on either side of this room's bed accomplish two goals. First, they provide ample storage for books and other necessities. Second, thanks to a slim profile and a paint color that matches the floor, they are hardly visible, adding to the spare look of the space.

▼ INSTALL A NIGHTSTAND with drawers so that you can easily conceal books, magazines, knitting supplies, and other potential clutter from view.

Closets and Dressing Rooms

I F YOU'RE LUCKY, EVEN YOUR SMALLEST BEDROOM has a closet of some sort where you can keep your clothes. The problem is, most closets, whether a narrow reach-in or a generous walk-in, are ill-equipped to handle the wardrobes we expect to stuff in them. The result? Clothing ends up piled on the floor or on a bedside chair. But it doesn't have to be this way. You can make small changes that will yield big benefits. For example, a door-mounted rack can help get your shoes off the floor, and hanging sweater bags can give you additional shelf space without the hassle, or expense, of construction. With the right organizing solution, you can have a closet that will not only accommodate all of your clothing, shoes, and accessories but also will make it easier to put them away at night and find them again in the morning.

▲ THE SECRET TO TAMING UNRULY DRESSER DRAWERS: Outfit them with store-bought containers intended for office supplies. To determine the containers and quantity that you will need, sort your accessories into categories before heading to the store.

▲ CREATE A SEPARATE DRESSING AREA to prevent clothing from cluttering the bedroom. The space can be an entire room or a closet that is deep enough to walk into. If you don't have a walk-in space, purchase a rolling cart that fits inside your closet. When you need to get dressed, simply roll out the cart.

Clothing Measurements

Before purchasing a premade storage system, ensure a perfect fit by checking the dimensions of the various components against these common clothing measurements:

- Hats: 11 in. wide
- Handbags: 9 in. high
- Shirts, sport coats, and skirts: 38 in. long
- Dresses: 65 in. long
- Folded pants: 30 in. long
- Shoes: 12 in. deep
- Boots: 18 in. high

Essential Closet Organizers

If your closet is out of control, the following organizing products found at hardware stores and home centers can help you restore order. What's more, each of these products attaches directly to the closet's rod, so installation is a snap.

- Handbag file. Eight clear plastic sleeves attached to a single hanger. Each sleeve can accommodate one large bag or several smaller clutch styles.
- Pocket shoe bags. Similar in design to a handbag file, except each pocket holds a pair of shoes.
- Sweater bags. Vertical shelves designed to hold stacks of folded sweaters or shirts.
- Jewelry organizer. Clear vinyl bags that contain anywhere from 30 to 80 small pockets for organizing earrings, pins, and other small accessories.

◀ CONVERT A SMALL BEDROOM into a walk-in closet by installing kitchen-style cabinets, which can be purchased for very little money at any home center. The glass-fronted doors used to create this space are attractive and practical, protecting the contents from dust, while allowing the owner to see easily what's stored inside.

An Organized Adult's Closet

These recommendations from the National Closet Group can be used as a guide in configuring an adult's closet.

- 12 in. to 14 in. between sweater shelves (shelf depth: 16 in.)
- 6 in. between shoe shelves (shelf depth: 12 in. to 14 in.)
- For double-hanging rods, place top rod 80 in. high, allowing two sections of about 40 in.
- Depth: 24 in. for suits and dresses; 28 in. for coats
- 55 in. for medium-length garments
- 63 in. for long garments
- Belt hook: 50 in. from floor
- 40 in. for suits, shirts, and skirts

▲ IF NEAT PILES AREN'T YOUR FORTE, outfit closet shelves with lined baskets or covered boxes. Attach labels, or a Polaroid picture in the case of shoes, so that it's easy to find what you're looking for.

▲ THIS CONTEMPORARY CLOSET ARRANGEMENT pairs drawers and shelves in one wall-mounted unit. To organize this type of set up, use the shelf space for things that are currently in season and the drawer below for things that are not. Simply switch items when the seasons change.

► EVEN STANDARD-SIZE CLOSETS can be made more functional by replacing the usual single shelf and rod with a store-bought system made of either wood or wire. Before making a purchase, take inventory of what you own so you are sure to buy the right components, like bins or boxes for odd-shaped items.

▲ READY-MADE CLOSET ACCESSORIES like hanging shoe bags and covered boxes, which can be found at most major retail stores, offer a less expensive alternative to a complete custom redo.

Closet Cleanup

Here's how to organize your closet in five simple steps:

1. Empty the closet of all its contents.
2. Vacuum and dust the interior.
3. Sort clothing by categories: jackets, pants, skirts, dresses, shirts, shoes, and so forth. Give to charity anything you have not worn in at least a year.
4. Pick a category and start returning items from that group to the closet. Sort items that you are returning by season and color.
5. Once everything is in place, use permanent markers so you'll always know where something goes. For example, add decorative labels to the front of each shelf to delineate what's to be stored.

Bathrooms

LARGE OR SMALL, SHARED OR PRIVATE, bathrooms have undergone significant changes over the last several years. Utilitarian spaces are out and spa-like retreats are in. But in the rush to create a comfortable place to relax after a hard day at work, don't overlook the obvious. Towels and toiletries still need a place to call home. So do supplies like toilet paper and cleaning gear. If you have the room, many of these things can be hidden from view in cabinets or other freestanding containers. If not, you might need to convert a nearby closet to an auxiliary storage space, or add a wall-mounted medicine cabinet or a set of shelves that can accommodate deep storage baskets. The end result will be a bath in which spending time is blissful.

▼ THE SECRET TO SUCCESSFUL STORAGE is always to keep items in close proximity to where they are needed. Here, a wall of cubbies provides easy access for towels and other bathing supplies. But open storage isn't for everyone. If you're not meticulous about how things are put away, the room's "clean" look can quickly disappear.

◄ A SIMPLE SOLUTION FOR ORGANIZING TOWELS in a shared family bath: Install a rail with pegs and designate a peg for each person. Avoid confusion by either labeling the pegs with each family member's name or assigning each person a different color towel.

◄ IF BUILT-INS AREN'T TO YOUR LIKING, borrow an idea from Victorian homes and furnish the bath with freestanding furniture. Here, a stainless-steel bench and towel rack keep toiletries and fresh towels within close proximity to the tub.

▲ PEDESTAL SINKS ARE PRETTY, but they don't provide much space for storing grooming supplies. One way to remedy the situation is to mount a shelf over the sink. The least obtrusive options are glass designs. Another idea: Utilize the molding that caps the wainscoting behind the sink as a secondary storage shelf.

Essential Bathroom Organizers

The following accessories found at hardware stores and home centers can help bring order to your bathroom:

- **Clear jars or canisters.** Fill them with cotton balls, swabs, and other small items.
- **Drawer and cabinet organizers.** These square and rectangular containers are ideal for grouping tubes of toothpaste, cosmetics, and other small toiletries.
- **Hooks.** Perhaps the most versatile storage device, these can be mounted anywhere and used to hold a basket filled with hand soaps or a pocket organizer for sorting toiletries.
- **Shower caddies.** Use them to organize your bathing essentials such as soap, shampoo, and sponges.
- **Stackable bins.** If your bath lacks cabinets, these bins, which can be stacked in a corner or placed beneath a pedestal sink, can provide storage space.

▲ SMALL BATHROOMS call for creativity. Here, dead wall space was converted to a narrow set of built-in shelves sized to accommodate both towels and toiletries.

▲ IN THIS BATH, LESS IS MORE. With only a simple storage shelf over each sink, the owners have to carefully select what toiletries to store. The result: a bath that's spare but serene.

▲ THIS BATHROOM OWES its orderly appearance to a variety of storage solutions that provide a place for everything. Open shelves beneath the sink house towels, while cleaning products are concealed in a closed cabinet. The niche to the left of the mirror provides a place for toiletries, helping to reduce counter clutter.

◄ NO LINEN CLOSET? NO PROBLEM. Here, a wall-mounted coat rack with an upper storage shelf works wonders. The hooks that would normally hold coats and hats can be used for robes and wet towels. The shelf can be used to store fresh linens or even toiletries or supplies.

▼ INSTEAD OF USING A DOOR to separate the toilet from the rest of the bath, the designer of this space created a custom wall that incorporates a rack for reading material as well as a shelf for supplies. If custom isn't an option, you can create a similar solution by using a narrow, freestanding bookshelf.

QUICK FIX

Clean Up the Medicine Cabinet

Organize your medicine cabinet in five simple steps.

1. Take everything out of the cabinet.
2. Discard any expired prescriptions or toiletries that you no longer use.
3. Remove any duplicate or surplus items, and store them in an alternate place, like a linen closet.
4. Divide what's left into categories such as medications, oral hygiene, first aid, and shaving equipment. Place cotton balls and swabs into small jars or canisters that fit inside the cabinet.
5. Return everything to the cabinet, keeping like items together. If space permits, designate a shelf for each category. If not, divide shelves using plastic bins, grouping the contents of one category in each bin.

▲ TWO MEDICINE CABINETS can be better than one—especially in a shared bath. Not only do they create a balanced display, but with a cabinet for each person, counters stay cleaner because there's more space to stow things.

▲ WHEN THE TIME COMES TO FURNISH A BATH, think of the room as you would any other in your home. Instead of adding costly built-in cabinets, use furniture. A dresser with deep drawers can be used to keep both towels and toiletries tidy and out of sight.

▼ THE KEY TO KEEPING HARMONY in a shared space is to provide plenty of places for everyone's things. In this master bath, that meant installing two sinks with two mirrors separated by a narrow cabinet for storing soaps, toothpaste, and other shared supplies.

▲ THE SHELF IN THIS TUB AREA offers a great opportunity to display decorative bottles and dishware. Put those pieces to practical use by filling them with soap and shampoo. More shelves or a towel rack on the unused wall could replace the chair if you need floor space.

◄ THIS BATH'S LADDER-STYLE STORAGE UNIT is in keeping with the room's clean appearance. The frameless mirror mounted over the sink conceals a deep storage cabinet, allowing for a contemporary counter-less sink. And because the sink is wall mounted, there's plenty of extra space below for bins or a rolling cabinet should extra storage be required.

◄ IN THIS SMALL BATH, every bit of space is used to best advantage, from the wall-mounted towel bars to the bench and storage ledge around the bathtub.

▲ ALWAYS MOUNT HOOKS for hand towels near the sink so guests can easily find them. Place a basket below the sink to catch soiled cloths.

▲ MAKE YOUR LIFE EASY and put decorative surfaces to work. This large deck is a great place for towels. The handsome soap holder over the tub is as much decorative as it is practical.

Small Space Solutions

Maximize space in a powder room by using one of these inventive ideas:

- Keep only the supplies that you are presently using on hand. Place everything else in a closet outside the bathroom or on a shelf in the garage or basement.
- Install two standard-size towel bars or hooks on the back of the bathroom door for hanging towels and bathrobes.
- Utilize the area over the toilet for wall-mounted shelves. Make sure they are deep enough to accommodate standard-size toiletries.

- Outfit bathroom cabinets with stackable containers to corral toiletries and supplies. If the cabinet is deep enough, a door-mounted spice rack can accomplish the same purpose.
- Install a wall-mounted holder at the sink for toothbrushes and toothpaste. Add a hook for a hair dryer. In the shower, hang a storage caddy from the shower-head or install wall-mounted baskets or dispensers for soap and shampoo.

▲ THIS POWDER ROOM SHOWCASES a number of innovative ideas, like the wall-mounted wire basket used for towel storage. The deep molding installed around the perimeter of the space provides overflow storage for essential supplies.

Kids' Spaces

I n any household where children are present, you're certain to find toys, books, and clothing strewn throughout most rooms. Short of banishing kids to their own wing, there's little you can do to stop these small messes from occurring. What you can do, however, is make it easier for them to round up their belongings by selecting a range of age-appropriate storage solutions. For example, if your children are elementary age or younger, provide rolling carts and baskets with handles that are easy for small hands to lift and tote to a designated spot. Once your child has graduated from building blocks and dolls to computer games and music, assign a shelf for their belongings. Binders with plastic sleeves can be used to store CDs, while small baskets can contain video games.

The same technique can be applied to clothing and shoes. A closet that functions best for a child has plenty of shelves that can be adjusted to his level or baskets that can simply be set on the floor. Although rods should also be included, don't expect young children to hang up clothes without assistance.

And don't forget homework. Avoid a pileup of book bags, papers, pencils, and other study supplies at the kitchen table by creating a dedicated workspace in your child's room.

◀ ROOMS EXCLUSIVELY DEVOTED TO THE ACTIVITIES OF CHILDREN don't have to be chaotic. Here, open shelving and closed storage units provide ample space for organizing supplies such as computer paper, reference books, and art materials. At the same time, two desks clearly define work and arts-and-crafts areas, keeping like-supplies contained in the appropriate space.

Bedrooms

KIDS' BEDROOMS OFTEN WEAR MULTIPLE HATS, operating as a playroom, study area, and sleeping space. Given the many functions that these rooms perform, some chaos can be expected, but too much can make it difficult for even the most spacious rooms to perform any one purpose well. The solution, short of moving one or two of the activities to another area of the house, is organizing the space to meet your child's many needs. Improving the room's storage by adding a flexible shelving system along one wall can easily help you accomplish this goal. This would free up valuable floor space so your child has room to play or so you have a place to add a small table for homework or craft projects. Similarly, lofting an older child's bed can afford you the space required to add a desk below, thus creating a secluded study area. In either case, flexibility and efficient storage are the keys to creating a multifunctional space.

▲ IF YOUR CHILD'S ROOM lacks sufficient closet space, create a small freestanding storage space using ready-to-assemble cabinetry from a home center. Covering two facing pantry-style cabinets with a piece of painted plywood formed this enclosed area. A simple hinged door gives the unit a finished look and hides everything inside from sight.

◀ THE BED IN THIS ROOM is framed with a wall of built-in shelves that provide easy-access storage for toys and books. Those shelves that aren't within the child's reach are used to display breakable items. The empty space over the bed is perfect for showcasing a child's work of art.

◄ EVERY KID LIKES TO HAVE her artwork and other fun stuff in her bedroom. These simple shelves are high enough on the wall to keep little fingers away from breakables but allow for an organized display of cherished mementos and artwork.

▲ HANGERS ARE DIFFICULT for little hands to use. To make a kid-friendly closet, use hanging bags with clear pockets. This way kids only have to tuck things inside and contents are easily identified.

THE PROS KNOW

Take advantage of the empty space below your child's bed. Measure the area, noting not only depth and width but also height. Then store appropriately sized containers such as baskets and shallow bins underneath.

◄ PULL OUT BINS, like this one, installed no more than 36 in. from the floor make it easy for a child to store dirty clothes.

Space-Saving Beds

In small spaces, like a child's bedroom, it is particularly important that space is used efficiently. And if your child's room is like most, the bed is probably the one furniture item that encompasses the largest amount of usable space. To that end, consider a model that has lots of built-in shelves and drawers. Here are a few favorite styles:

- **Loft systems.** These are one of the best solutions for space-starved rooms. Look for configurations that feature shelves, drawers, a desk, and a cupboard and act as a bed, closet, and work center all in one.

- **Trundle beds.** Because the second mattress slides under the primary bed frame, these twin-size designs are a perfect solution for rooms that require, but can't accommodate, two units.

- **Captain's beds.** Lower than a loft but taller than a standard twin, this popular children's bed features a bank of drawers or shelves below the mattress.

- **Headboards.** Think of these kid-friendly beds as modified bookcases with storage for everything from a reading light to reading material.

▲ ONE WAY TO ENSURE that your child's room retains a neat and tidy appearance is to contain all of the storage and function in one area of the room using a single piece of furniture. This custom bed with a built-in dresser serves multiple functions.

▲ SIZE YOUR STORAGE TO FIT what it is you're stowing. For example, when outfitting a nursery, use an armoire rather than a traditional closet. Because its proportions are smaller than most closets, an armoire can perfectly accommodate infant clothing.

► PEGBOARD USED in this girl's bedroom is an inexpensive and kid-friendly way to keep dolls, books, and toys organized.

◄ LOOKING FOR AN EASY WAY to organize your child's shoes? Consider a vinyl rack with adjustable bins, like this one, which can be mounted on the inside of most closet doors.

▼ IF YOUR CHILD IS A SPORTS ENTHUSIAST, consider making the collection part of the décor. Here, simple wall-mounted rods keep a selection of sports jerseys and bats in order. A narrow shelf overhead provides space for balls and trophies.

▼ ORGANIZING A SPACE SHARED BY TWO CHILDREN can be a challenge. Here, a custom bunk-bed unit solves that dilemma. It includes two of everything, including the notice boards and reading lights. The built-in shelves are a nice feature for stowing bedtime reading when it's time for lights out.

A Closet That Works

A child's closet can be configured much like your own. Once you take inventory of its contents, shop home centers for hanging rods, wire or wood shelves, and baskets that will fit the space.

When you arrange the closet, consider your child's age and size. To encourage your children to hang up their clothes, rods should be mounted so that they are within reach. If space permits, install two rods—one up high for dress clothes and off-season things and a lower rod for everyday items. Instead of drawers, opt for shelves. They're easier for little ones to use—especially with folded clothing.

Finally, if two children share a closet, divide it in two, then make sorting simple by labeling each child's shelves, baskets, and other storage devices.

► WHEN ARRANGING A NURSERY, think in terms of zones. Here, a changing station was created by simply adding a table with shelves for storing diapers, clothes, and blankets. A shelf with hooks provides a convenient place to hang outfits as well as store essential items such as baby lotion and powder.

THE PROS KNOW

Simplify your child's morning routine by selecting what will be worn to school the night before. Mount a hook inside the closet door and hang the outfit there so come morning, getting dressed is easy.

▶ LOCKER-STYLE CABINETS, like these, are ideal furnishings for rooms shared by two or more kids. Add one for each occupant so they have a private place to stash their personal belongings.

▼ THIS IS THE EPITOME of a well-organized closet, with dedicated spaces for hanging and folded clothes and wall-mounted bins for odd-shaped items. Shoes can fit neatly on the floor.

Creating a Room That Grows

When selecting furnishings for children, avoid investing in major pieces that have a theme. For example, resist the urge to buy your toddler a train-shaped toy chest, even if he's passionate about trains. Interests change and all too soon, your son may be on to race cars or even airplanes. Instead, select a plain painted box that can grow with him from preschool through primary school.

▲ THE RIGHT FURNISHINGS can make organizing a child's belongings easier. This bench provides both a comfortable place to sit as well as easy-to-access storage for shoes and books.

◄ NOT ONLY DOES THIS SMALL BEDROOM have a place for everything, but it's also arranged so that the work area is separate from the sleeping space. To make the most of the tight quarters, clever storage opportunities abound, from the deep drawers below the mattress to the shelves over the bed and desk.

► THIS COLORFUL, THEMED ROOM offers lots of storage options, from the shelves for toys and books to the peg rack for hats and a dresser with multiple drawers. The radiator cover with shelf is a bonus.

An Organized Child's Closet

These recommendations from the National Closet Group can be used as a guide in configuring a child's closet.

- Depth: 24 in.
- 26 in. for triple-hung clothing (ages 3 to 5)
- 40 in. for double-hung clothing (ages 6 to 12)
- 55 in. for long garments
- Belt hook: 42 in. from the floor

Homework Helpers

I T'S A FACT: ORGANIZATION AND GOOD STUDY HABITS go hand in hand. It's also easier for children to focus on homework when the area they're working in is both orderly and equipped with whatever tools they need. Begin with the work surface. Place a sturdy desk or table (one that's large enough to accommodate a computer and printer) in a part of the house that is removed from the activity and noise of the main living spacezs. If the desk lacks adequate storage for supplies, add a rolling cart with baskets or drawers that can be used to organize paper, pencils, and other necessities. If the desk and computer are to be shared by more than one child, use rolling carts (one for each child) to sort books and supplies. This will allow them to easily transport their belongings when it's their turn to use the desk.

▲ TO MAINTAIN ORDER ON A DESKTOP, group supplies as well as reading materials in colorful containers. To keep the primary work surface clear, consider a desk with a hutch that has shelves located over the work surface or install your own shelving unit near the work surface.

◄ HOMEWORK IS MUCH EASIER TO COMPLETE when a child has a dedicated place to do it. Here, a simple desk made of white laminate provides space for two. The shelf that divides the work surface is both a whimsical and practical addition, providing each child with a conveniently located shelf to stash supplies.

◄ THIS SIMPLE FURNITURE ARRANGEMENT contains everything a child needs to study—a solid work surface, drawers for supplies, and open shelves for reference books.

▲ ORGANIZE THE INSIDE OF A CHILD'S DESK the same way you would your own. Use colorful plastic bins to sort supplies like scissors, pencils, and erasers. Set up hanging files in which to keep school papers. To maintain order, sort through files at the end of each school year, saving only papers of significant importance.

Create an Activity Center

To encourage creativity but control the mess it can leave in its wake, designate an arts-and-crafts area in your home. Doing so will minimize the number of crayons, scissors, and paper scraps you find scattered throughout the house. Here are a few suggestions of what to include:

- A child-size table and set of chairs.
- A bookshelf or cabinet lined with handled storage bins for stashing art supplies.
- An easel and a blackboard.
- Protective gear like smocks and table covers.
- Large containers for stashing cardboard, empty boxes, and other inspirational supplies.
- Jars or plastic containers for paintbrushes, pens, pencils, and chalk.

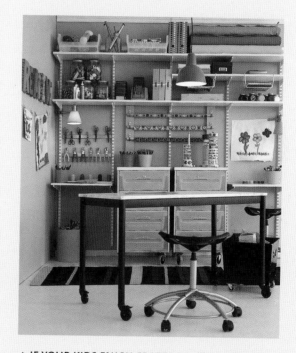

▲ IF YOUR KIDS ENJOY CRAFTS, you'll want a dedicated place for them to produce things. To that end, convert a corner of a basement into a crafter's paradise by lining the walls with adjustable shelves for stowing bulky supplies. Simple see-through plastic drawers can be used to keep smaller supplies tidy.

Saving Memories

Most young children bring home at least one art project a week that winds up on the refrigerator. But what becomes of these masterpieces once they've worn out their welcome in the kitchen? Easy. Place one or two favorites in permanent frames that you hang or display in a specific part of the house. Stash the remainder in a flat file box or cabinet with multiple drawers that are wide enough to easily accommodate oversized art papers. And be sure to select a cabinet with several drawers so you can stash more than a year's worth of work.

▼ CONVERTING THIS BEDROOM ALCOVE into a dedicated study space was simple. The only things needed were a sturdy desk and chair. A shelving unit mounted over the top of the desk provides a convenient place to organize reading and reference materials.

Storing Craft Supplies

Arts and crafts and kids go hand in hand. Here are four inventive ideas for organizing all of the supplies required for a well-stocked art center.

◄ SMALL ITEMS LIKE BUTTONS and beads are best organized by color and style, then stowed in cases normally used for watch or jewelry parts.

► DISCARD THE PACKAGING for all of your crayons, markers, and pencils. Stow these materials in colorful and easy-to-use ceramic flowerpots.

◄ FIND A NEW USE for ordinary household equipment. Here, paper-towel holders are used to keep rolls of ribbon and stickers in order.

► A SIMPLE SILVERWARE CADDY can be adapted as an easy-to-carry box for scrapbooking supplies like rubber stamps and craft punches.

▲ WHEN POSSIBLE, cordon off an alcove as a dedicated space for a child, even if it's in her bedroom. You'll find that the child is more likely to keep the space neat and tidy if she thinks of it as her own.

Play Spaces

ANY PARENT KNOWS HOW EASY IT IS FOR toys to take over the house. But it's equally easy to make sure they are put away. The secret is providing children with simple but sturdy storage solutions. A plastic bin on wheels, for example, can easily be transported from room to room to gather toys. When all of the items have been collected, the bin can be returned to its designated spot. Or buy baskets with handles and line them up on a low shelf where they're easy for kids to grab and tote to another room in the house.

If your home has a spare room available, establish a playroom that your children can use with their friends. A dedicated space will help contain clutter in one specific area, making it easier for you and your children to keep a handle on their toys. Install a storage system that utilizes both open and closed shelving so there's a place for everything and everything ends up in its proper place.

▲ OPEN BINS are one of the best organizing tools for toys. Why? Because they're easy for little hands to reach into and take things out or put things away.

◄ A STURDY SET OF SHELVES can keep more than a child's personal library in line. It can also be used for getting small toys off the floor. Simply outfit the shelf with baskets sized to fit the space.

THE PROS KNOW

Want your kids to clean up? Make them part of the solution by having them help you select the storage containers that will be used to contain all of their gear. Perhaps they can suggest the colors for the bins or make drawings for the labels that will indicate what's inside.

◄ STYLISH STORAGE doesn't have to be expensive. Here, simple wire shelves have been fitted with a custom fabric cover to make them more suitable for a child's room. Pockets sewn to the outside of the cover are sized to accommodate oversized picture books and art supplies.

▲ OUTFITTING A CLOSET with stackable baskets that rest on the floor makes the space easier for a child to use. Lidded containers, sized to fit the dimensions of the baskets, can further organize the space.

► FIND A NEW USE for a standard storage product. Here, an over-the-door shoe caddy keeps Ken, Barbie, and all of their clothes and accessories in order. Pictograph labels make it easy for a young child to understand what's stowed where.

▲ WHEN PLANNING PLAYROOM STORAGE, don't overlook the odd alcove. Here, shallow shelves were built into unused wall space. The bench opens to hide away toys and books, and baskets hold the overflow.

Perfecting Playroom Storage

The first step in bringing order to the playroom is weeding out unwanted or outgrown toys and donating them to charity. Once this has been accomplished, consider a variety of storage containers. Here are a few favorites:

- Plastic jars. These are perfect for puzzle pieces and other toys with small parts. Because the jars are clear, identifying the contents is easy.
- Multicompartment shoe bags. Hang one on the back of a closet door, and use it to organize stuffed animals and dolls.
- Metal or plastic buckets. Fill these with toys, like beach gear, that your child may want to take elsewhere.
- Baskets and bins. Because these storage solutions have no lids, they're easy for little ones to fill.
- Shelves. Use either freestanding or built-in designs to keep all of the jars, baskets, and storage bins in order.

◄ WHEN PLANNING YOUR CHILD'S playroom, borrow an idea from the garage. Outfit a wall with pegboard, then use it to organize kid-size kitchenware and other toys that are otherwise difficult to store.

▲ THE BEAUTY OF SMALL WOODEN SHELVES, like these, is that they can be placed just about anywhere additional storage is needed. Hang them over a work surface and use them to organize art supplies, or place them next to a favorite chair where they can accommodate a selection of books.

▼ TO ENCOURAGE CLEANUP, every playroom needs at least one storage cart with wheels. Designs with clear plastic bins make it easy for kids to see where things should go.

How to Get Kids to Clean Up

The chances of having a child who doesn't leave toys scattered across the living room are slim. Kids, after all, will be kids. But that doesn't mean you have to clean up after them. The trick: Make them understand at an early age that cleaning can be fun by using the following ideas.

- Make a game out of it. Turn toy cleanup into a game of "I Spy," asking them to locate and put away specific toys.
- Keep it simple. Make it easy for your child to make his own bed by keeping blankets and covers to a minimum.
- Whistle while you work. Lead your children in singing a silly song as they help you tidy up the playroom.

Stackable cubes made of plastic or light-weight wood are one of the best shelving storage options for small children because they are simple to set up and rearrange.

▲ EVERY PLAYROOM SHOULD BE EQUIPPED with open containers like this mesh folding crate. Lined up against a wall, they simplify the cleanup process to one that involves little more than tossing toys in the appropriate container. And because the containers are not opaque, kids can easily find what they're looking for.

▶ WHEN CHOOSING A STORAGE SYSTEM for your child's toys, look for one that can grow in size. Here, stacked cubes, which are small and lightweight, can easily be reconfigured and added to as storage needs change.

▲ KEEPING TRACK OF SMALL ITEMS like game and puzzle pieces can be difficult, especially if a box breaks down. Avoid losing these parts by storing them in small plastic containers, which will fit in standard dresser drawers for easy storage. For a low-tech version, use empty egg crates, shallow cardboard boxes, or silverware storage trays.

▲ BECAUSE IT'S OPEN and easy to dig through, a wheeled basket, like this, is ideal for storing an abundance of dress up clothes, toys, or even shoes.

► KEEP BOOKS, ESPECIALLY THOSE FROM THE LIBRARY, on a dedicated shelf. Not only does this prevent them from getting lost, but it also protects them from damage that could result if they were left on the floor. To make sure library books are returned on time, attach a list with their due dates above one of the shelves.

Workspaces

Utilitarian spaces seldom receive the attention they deserve—an ironic twist of fate when you consider that the rooms falling into this category, like a home office, laundry room, and garage, are some of the hardest-working areas in our homes.

For many families, the one thing that makes organizing these areas so difficult is the simple fact that they're often not self-contained rooms but shared spaces—the laundry room that resides in a corner by the back door or the home office located in a corner in the kitchen.

In places like these, storage systems might be haphazardly thrown together, if they exist at all. To fix the problem, you don't need elaborate, expensive solutions. But you do need to make efficient use of the space for the stuff you want to store now—and in the future. With a little forethought and creativity, you can convert these humdrum areas of the home into efficient spaces that help make your life run more smoothly.

◀ PROPERLY OUTFITTED, A LAUNDRY ROOM can house more than a washer and dryer. It can also contain all of your household's cleaning gear. Ready-to-assemble cabinets like these are widely available at home centers and discount stores. Remove shelves to accommodate bulky cleaning equipment and supplies.

Home Offices

HOME OFFICES ARE NO LONGER JUST FOR paying bills and writing letters. Today these busy spaces do triple duty, providing a spot for managing household paperwork, doing homework and activities with the kids, and actually working from home. Of course, the organizing system you adopt here depends largely on the type of space you have. If your office is a separate room, for instance, you'll have more flexibility for utilizing storage units and filing cabinets. However, if it's a cordoned-off corner of the living room, traditional office furniture may not be the best (or most attractive) option. Instead, you may need to devise a more creative solution that encompasses built-ins or some other type of attractive storage. In either case, the key to designing a well-organized office is understanding how you and your family will use the space and how hard it needs to work for you.

▲ SIMPLE GLASS CONTAINERS make standard office supplies like rubber bands, paper clips, and even pens appear more attractive. Plus they're easy to find and get when needed.

▼ WHEN ORGANIZING YOUR HOME OFFICE, don't overlook the wall space above your desktop. Use this area to mount a bulletin board that can be used to post both a calendar and important reminders.

◄ HERE'S AN EASY WAY to maintain a tidy desktop. Use a large tray to contain the small boxes and canisters that hold supplies like paper clips, pencils, and notepads.

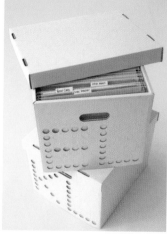

▲ INSTEAD OF LITTERING YOUR DESKTOP with an array of plastic containers, look for storage that reflects your personal style. Here, a repurposed card catalog provides plenty of hiding places for stamps, paper clips, rubber bands, and other office essentials.

Bulletin Board Basics

Not only do bulletin boards make keeping track of appointments and invitations easy, but also they provide a convenient place to post bills and messages. To create a board that complements your office, use one of the following techniques:

- Mount galvanized metal panels over a work area and use decorative magnets.
- Cover a wall with fabric-wrapped cork panels.
- Finish a closet door with magnetic chalkboard paint so you can write directly on it and post reminders.
- Frame a fabric-covered board, then hang it on a wall or rest it on an easel.

▲ THE SECRET TO A SUCCESSFUL FILING SYSTEM is to keep on hand only the things you need on a daily basis. Everything else should be packed away in boxes, like these, that can be easily retrieved if their contents are required. Before stowing, label each box with your initials and a description of what's inside.

If you have extensive files or are placing important documents in deep storage in your attic or basement, create a directory, or list of files, so you know where to find paperwork should you need to retrieve it at a later date.

▲ SIMPLE CANVAS BINS are an easy and attractive way to organize piles of papers. Designate one bin per project or activity and place the bins on shelves so they are out of the way.

◄ SUPPLIES THAT ARE USED REGULARLY should be kept in the open so they're always within easy reach. Here, a collection of old jars and bottles containing an assortment of paint brushes could just as well hold pens and pencils, scissors, rulers, and letter openers.

The Paper Chase

Before you can establish an efficient filing system, you must decide what to keep and what to toss. Begin by gathering all of your paperwork in one place. Then start sorting that one gigantic pile into smaller, more manageable stacks. Here is a quick rundown of what to keep and what to toss.

Keep

- Birth and death certificates
- Health records
- Insurance policies
- Marriage, divorce, adoption, and other official papers
- Mortgage and loan papers (discard 3 years after the loan is paid in full)
- Passports
- Property deeds
- Receipts and warranties for appliances
- Stock and bond certificates
- Tax records (keep business records for seven years; personal records for four years)
- Wills

Discard

- Magazine and newspaper articles and clippings that you haven't referred to in several years
- ATM and deposit slips after they have been recorded in your checkbook
- Bank and credit card statements more than 1 year old
- Business cards you no longer need
- Expired coupons
- Old receipts (unless you itemize your taxes)
- Pay stubs at the end of the calendar year and after you have completed your taxes

▲ KEEP TABS ON EXPENDITURES and save time preparing your taxes by sorting your receipts on a weekly basis. A small box with tabs or an accordion file will do the trick.

▲ WHEN STORING OFFICE DOCUMENTS, consider utilizing clear plastic bins so that contents are clearly visible. Storing the bins on glide-out shelves, normally used in kitchens, makes finding what you need even easier since you don't have to pull out the box and set it down.

▲ ORGANIZATIONAL TOOLS designed to bring order to other parts of your house can also be used to organize your office. Here, kitchen-style cabinet pullouts allow the printer, fax, and hard drive to be hidden when not in use.

◀ YOU DON'T NEED a dedicated room in order to have a well-ordered workspace. This clever computer station is actually in a kitchen. When not in use, the computer, which resides on a pullout shelf, disappears into a cabinet.

Alternative Offices

If you don't have a separate room to use as an office, consider one of the following options:

- **Armoire.** Look for a unit that has already been outfitted with a fold-down writing surface and keyboard tray, or find a unit at a flea market with a deep interior that can be easily adapted.
- **Reach-in closet.** Remove the rod and any lower shelves. Then add a file cabinet and a piece of wood that has been cut to fit the closet's width and depth. If needed, add shelves over the work surface to provide storage for books and file boxes. Bonus: When you're finished working, you can just shut the door.
- **Folding screen.** Cordon off a corner in the living room or another shared space and use this to hide a desk and shelves.

▲ CONVERTING AN UNUSED CLOSET into a home office is easy. Simply outfit the space with a simple desk and shelves sized to hold baskets or file boxes. Have an electrician add an outlet or two so there's a place to plug in a computer and reading lamp.

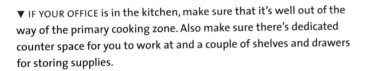

▼ IF YOUR OFFICE is in the kitchen, make sure that it's well out of the way of the primary cooking zone. Also make sure there's dedicated counter space for you to work at and a couple of shelves and drawers for storing supplies.

▲ COMPUTER ARMOIRES are an ideal office solution when space is tight. Just make sure that the armoire you choose is configured with a shelving system that can accommodate your needs. Another idea: Select an empty armoire and have a carpenter create a custom interior that will accommodate all of your office gear.

▶ ONE WAY TO ENSURE your desk stays clear of clutter is to surround the work surface with plenty of built-in cubbies. To maintain order, give each cubby a specific purpose, like mail, bills, and correspondence.

Laundry Rooms

I F YOU'RE LIKE MOST PEOPLE, you probably dislike spending time sequestered in the laundry room. After all, let's face it, washing, folding, and ironing clothes are all mundane tasks. But spending time in this bland area of the home is much easier if the space is tidy and orderly. To improve your wash-day outlook, break the laundry room down into individual zones organized around specific tasks—in this case, spaces for sorting, washing, folding, and ironing. Then equip each area with the proper tools for the task. Key elements include shelves for storing detergent and other supplies, a utility sink for clothing that needs to be washed by hand, a rack or clothesline for drying, and an adequate counter for folding and sorting.

▲ A LAUNDRY ROOM CAN ALSO DOUBLE as a utility space. To convert yours, simply follow this idea and outfit a wall with pegboard. Small S-shaped hooks or simple two-prong brackets will keep mops, brooms, dustpans, and other cleaning essentials well organized and out of the way.

◄ STACKING LAUNDRY EQUIPMENT allows you to convert any corner or closet into a well-ordered space for wash. Look for accessories, like a pullout wall-mounted drying rack, that can easily disappear when not in use.

▲ IF YOUR LAUNDRY AREA DOUBLES as your linen closet, make sure there are plenty of shelves for storing fresh towels and linens away from the cleaning supplies. Stowing front-loading equipment under a laminate or solid-surface counter will aid when folding and sorting.

THE PROS KNOW

Make shelves over or near the washer and dryer open so that it's quick to grab detergent and bleach when doing laundry and easy to see when you're running out of laundry supplies.

To simplify the task of doing laundry, place labeled portable receptacles (either baskets or bags) in each family member's bedroom or bath. When the receptacle is full, the family member can carry it to the laundry room.

▲ THIS LAUNDRY ROOM KEEPS AN ABUNDANCE of supplies neatly hidden. The vertical cabinets hide bulk cleaning supplies and provide a place for fresh towels and linens, while open shelving keeps detergent and other essential supplies within easy reach. A small table offers a nearby surface for sorting and folding clothes.

Contain It

Make your laundry room more appealing by repackaging essential supplies like laundry soap, fabric softener, and clothespins in decorative containers with the contents clearly marked. Utilize the following favorites:

- Lidded glass jars in a variety of shapes and sizes
- Colored glass or plastic bottles
- Stainless-steel kitchen or bathroom canisters
- Vintage cookie jars
- Plastic boxes with colored lids

▲ WOODEN PEGS ARE A HANDSOME WAY to add functionality to any laundry area. Use them to hang clothing items that must be air-dried. In this bright space, the shelf above the pegs is used to keep extra cleaning supplies within easy reach.

▲ THERE'S NO REASON WHY the laundry room can't be attractive. Empty the contents of unsightly detergent boxes into large, lidded glass containers that you can arrange neatly on a shelf.

▲ WHETHER YOUR WASH AREA is large or small, take advantage of what would otherwise be unused space. Here, two rods were installed above a small sink, while hooks were added beside it. Both areas are ideal for hanging items that you don't want to place in the dryer.

Create a Simple Sewing Space

A charming and functional sewing space will make mending clothes feel like less of a chore. Include a wall-mounted rack to keep thread organized and within reach. To keep supplies orderly, utilize mason jars or plastic boxes with built-in dividers for buttons, thimbles, patches, and other small items.

▼ STORING SPOOLS OF THREAD on a wall-mounted rack makes it easier to find the color you need to mend clothing.

▲ EVERY LAUNDRY ROOM should be equipped with hanging space for clothes that can't go in the dryer. Here, the rod was mounted over the sink, a clever move that not only conserves space, but also ensures that water won't drip all over the floor.

▲ IF YOU DON'T HAVE SPACE for a wall-mounted storage system, keep all of your sewing supplies in a basket that's stored on a shelf in the laundry room.

◄ FRONT-LOADING APPLIANCES allow laundry equipment to be stowed under a counter that offers plenty of elbow room for folding. They also make it possible to hide equipment in a hallway closet behind closed doors. Mount wire shelves over the laundry equipment to keep cleaning supplies close at hand.

◄ SIMPLIFY THE SORTING PROCESS by using a separate basket for each family member's laundry. Choose one color for dirty clothes and another for clean. Install a bank of shelves in the laundry room to stow the baskets.

Garages

I N MANY HOMES, THE GARAGE IS A DUMPING GROUND—a jumbled mess of everything that won't fit elsewhere in the house. Converting this disorganized area into a hardworking, functional space doesn't have to be difficult. You can, for example, reinstall old kitchen cabinets and use them to keep bulk buys in order until they are needed. Pegboard can be added to the walls to hang equipment and tools. You can also take advantage of ceiling space by adding hooks for bikes, canoes, kayaks, and other large sports gear. If shelving is required, home centers and discount stores carry a wide variety of inexpensive wire, metal, and wood designs. The key is corralling large like items and keeping everything else in containers or cabinets that make it easy to identify what's inside.

▲ INSTALL FLOOR-TO-CEILING SHELVING in your garage and soon the space will look as orderly as the rest of your house. Adjustable shelves will allow for maximum flexibility. Use plastic crates to contain smaller items to keep them from spilling onto the floor.

◀ GIVE OLD KITCHEN CABINETS a new lease on life by reusing them in a garage workshop. Set an old sturdy door (or buy an inexpensive one at your local home center) atop base cabinets to create a workbench. Use wall cabinets and pegboard to organize tools, nails, screws, and other hardware supplies.

◀ WALL-MOUNTED RACKS, like this one, are ideal space savers in garages that already have difficulty accommodating a car. Because these systems are modular, they can be easily altered as storage needs change.

▼ STACKING BINS, like these, can bring order to a garage that also doubles as a mudroom. Use them for shoes, umbrellas and other items that would otherwise end up in the way.

► PEGBOARD IS PERFECT for keeping tools organized and handy. Group tools by function and keep those most frequently used at eye level.

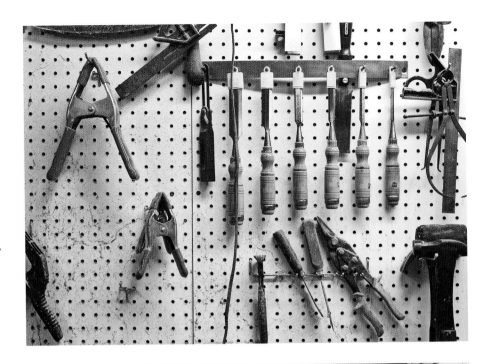

▼ THERE'S NO EXCUSE for a messy garage—especially when you consider all of the organizing systems available today. Wall-mounted rack systems work wonders when it comes to getting ladders and wheelbarrows out the way. Locking cabinets should be used to keep cleaning supplies, paints, and other materials away from kids.

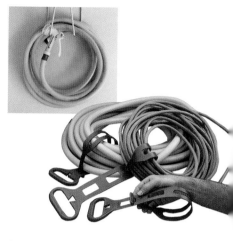

▲ HOOKS OF ALL KINDS can be hung on the garage wall to help keep cords, ropes, and hoses from being a coiled mess on the floor.

▲ WHEN IT COMES TO CONVERTING THE GARAGE, divide the space into zones. Allocate one area for sports equipment, and outfit it with ready-to-assemble cabinets available at home centers. A horizontal rack will keep hard-to-contain items like balls in place; a storage bench allows a place to sit while changing shoes.

▲ CEILING-MOUNTED RACKS, like these, help you maximize storage. Use them to organize seasonal gear or items that you don't need access to on a regular basis. Securing bikes to a wall mounted rack system ensures that they don't end up in the way.

Storage Basics

There are so many stories we all can tell about storage gone awry, yet we'd rather spend time choosing new window treatments than reconfiguring the front hall closet. Storage just doesn't get the respect it deserves. But just consider how much better it would be to take the time spent looking for misplaced stuff and to spend it on family, friends, hobbies, travel—on getting an extra half hour with a cup of coffee instead of frantically searching for the left shoe of the only pair that matches the suit you need for an important presentation, which you're now running late for.

Well-designed storage is completely subjective—what works well with one person's lifestyle could be disastrous for another. There's certainly no one way to achieve storage Zen, but there are some basic approaches and guidelines that will help demystify the process of creating good storage.

Storage Design 101

The first trick to efficient storage is to take a close look at how you store your things, and figure out what's wrong with your system and what works—and why. This may seem like a monumental bore at first, if not an impossibility. The very word *storage* is dull (it rhymes with *porridge* and *forage*—there's just no glamour in that), but storage is essential to living comfortably, and if it's designed well, storage can be a source of pleasure, too. Consider how pleasing it is to see and use a beautiful pot rack laden with copper saucepans or an armoire filled with soft bath towels.

To get to the core of what you can fix about your own storage, it helps to start thinking like a product designer. Brainstorm about the qualities of the items you want to store (this is a great project for kids working on "invention convention" assignments). Can the item drape or be hung from some-

◀**If there's a space for everything, there's a likelihood that everything will be in its place when** you need it. When a sporting season ends, make sure that long-term storage can handle all the appropriate gear until the season rolls around again. This handsome mudroom keeps clothing and gear in one place.

◄**Storing books, photos, and papers** is hardly a dull task in this handsome study. A blanket chest-cum-coffee table provides long-term storage for professional journals.

▲**This beautiful Craftsman-style cabinetry,** which is both built-in and freestanding, contains stationery and other odds and ends, and displays period vases and glass work.

thing without losing its shape? (Think scarves or a dog leash.) Or is it rounded and prone to rolling when set down so that it needs a basket? (Onions and marbles come to mind.) Can the item stand up and fit into a slot (envelopes and trays) or does it need to be stored flat (printer paper)?

A trip to the mall is another good way to start thinking about storage. Visit well-organized stores, and pay attention to how they display and store items. Chain stores often have some of the most ingenious storage systems, because they pay product designers a lot of money to come up with efficient and attractive storage for all of their locations. Of course, home storage differs in scale from the commercial, and translating commercial storage ideas into the home variety can be tricky.

Home-storage design is a booming business these days, but despite the vast number of products on the market, not all are created equal. You'd think that all storage products would be designed to be useful, but it isn't always so. When you find a product or system that appeals to you, visualize yourself actually using it; if you can picture the easy retrieval and return of items, then it's probably worth a shot. But if you foresee a lot of rooting around to find what you're looking for or knocking over other items in the process of getting what you want, look for a better solution.

Store Like Items Together—Usually

Take a look, too, at what items you store together. Generally speaking, it's easier to remember where everything is if you store

like items together. However, this rule only makes sense if it suits the way you live. Take spice storage, for instance. If you're a fan of red pepper and use it nightly at the stovetop, why store it in the pantry among a zillion other jars and bottles? If you blow-dry your hair in the dressing room, it makes no sense to store the blow-dryer in the bathroom with all the other grooming products. Keep in mind that this is a strictly subjective notion, as one person's taxonomy is another's nonsense. You may prefer all your ducks in a row, but your daughter may like her stuffed animals placed in a pattern that fits her sensibility, not your sense of order.

It's also possible that you'll find two equally compelling places to store an item. Instead of constantly wondering which place you have put it, why not store two of them? Have salt and pepper by the stovetop and by the sandwich-making countertop. If kids brush teeth downstairs in the morning and upstairs at night, supply two sets, with the downstairs set easy to whisk away when company calls.

▲ This view from the master bedroom shows a passage to the main floor flanked by a bathroom to the left and a dressing room to the right. Although the space reflects a minimalist approach, storage space is not sacrificed. Low, open shelves hold shoes, while wall-hung cabinets with open cubbies provide storage in both the bathroom and dressing space.

serious cooks contains a complete wet bar with an under-cabinet wine cooler, an ice machine, and cabinetry with glassware and dinnerware. Spices, condiments, and small tools used for making drinks (paring knives and zesters, for example) are kept in the tiny drawers, while spices for cooking are kept in the kitchen pantry and a duplicate set of small tools are kept in drawers near the cooktop.

If duplicating storage isn't in the cards, make mobile storage. Store items that are used in multiple places in a caddy, and put the caddy in a central location. For larger items, do the same with a rolling cart. For instance, if computer accessories are used with a laptop at the kitchen table and with a stationary computer in the study, store them on a rolling cart and position it in neutral territory, demanding that its contents be returned daily.

Consider Active versus Dead Storage

Well-placed storage makes it easier to handle daily, weekly, and periodical tasks. Before you settle on how to store your possessions, consider how often you use them. Objects that are used every day should be stored close by, perhaps in sight, while objects used weekly can be more remote but still be easy to reach. Everyday objects run the gamut from the small—dental floss and car keys—to larger items, such as kids'

▲ **This ladder is a permanent fixture, providing easy access** to the hatch, which leads to a brightly lit but low-ceilinged space perfect for out-of-season storage.

▼ **This hallway in a new Normandy-style** house does double duty as a passageway and a space for a stretch of beautiful mahogany cabinets, which provide ideal storage for seasonal items, extra linens, or even paperwork.

backpacks and bath towels. Items like this are considered "active" storage because they are constantly being used and put back or replenished. Active storage items must be easy to find and use, or efficiency is lost. A prime example is a set of car keys, which must be given an accessible and permanent home to keep mornings running smoothly.

But the items we use periodically need functional, accessible storage, too. Seasonal items—sports gear, clothing, decorations, and the like—need a consistent and designated place of rest. Call this "dead" storage, if you like, but its more like "dormant" stor-

age. The weeks before Christmas can seem like a year to a child but mere minutes to an adult who has to rummage through the closet looking for the box marked (or worse, not marked) "Christmas." Holiday decorations need a box (or more) and a dedicated spot in the basement, attic, spare closet, or any other convenient but out-of-the-way place.

Actual dead storage, which stays put for a very long time—a wedding dress, drawings and schoolwork from early childhood, vinyl records you can't bear to part with—can be stored quite far out of sight, but to keep

▲This stretch of cypress drawers, which runs the length of a Martha's Vineyard bedroom, conceals a lot of clothing while sitting low to allow an ocean view through awning windows.

them from being permanently out of mind, label storage containers well, and make a list of items and storage locations. When allocating long-term storage, also keep in mind safe storage environments. For instance, fragile items, such as keepsake papers and photos, should be stored in archival-quality boxes and albums and in a stable environment protected from extremes of heat and humidity.

Consider Concealed versus Open Storage

Another critical design task is to determine how much of your stuff you want to see every day. In a private space, such as a master bathroom, visible storage might include toothpaste, shaving gear, makeup, and other toiletries. In a more public bathroom downstairs, you might want to keep such items

out of sight. In the kitchen, personal preference frequently dictates storage design; some cooks prefer to keep cooking tools within easy reach on the countertop, while others like a minimalist look and have a drawer for everything.

Regardless of the room it's in, traditional cabinetry is often open at eye level and closed below, so that decorative objects are stored on the visible shelves—behind glass or not—and more utilitarian or less used objects are stored behind doors or in drawers below. This makes sense visually and offers the most flexible storage, but your personal style or storage needs may dictate that all cabinets are closed or open. It's your call. Just keep in mind that closed cabinets

◀**Built-in cabinetry can be** fitted with a mind-boggling variety of storage devices, making it easy to select the right storage solution. The entertainment portion of this Martha's Vineyard kitchen contains an under-counter wine cooler, diagonal cubbies for wine bottles, and an array of drawers, open shelves, glazed doors, and solid doors. All cabinetry is worked from reclaimed cypress. Oak trees that were cleared to make room for the house have been shaved, sanded, and joined to provide structural support.

shield items from dust and dirt, so if you're not a fan of dusting, a sea of open shelving may not be the most practical approach.

Match Storage to Items Stored

The apparatus that provides storage—a free-standing chest, a closet, a built-in hutch, or a wall-mounted rack—doesn't matter as much as the storage elements it contains. A closet can provide hooks, shelves, racks, and rods, but so can a built-in cabinet. It's important to take a close look at the items

you're storing and consider what will make the most effective storage device.

Shelves Shelves are one of the most versatile storage elements and are suitable for most of the things we store. Depending on whether they're open or hidden behind cabinet doors, shelves can accommodate everything from sculptures to books to extra toilet paper. The great benefit of open shelves is that they're easy and relatively inexpensive to add to a room, and just one

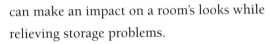

▲ **Light-as-air shelves hung from the ceiling provide two layers** of storage for a collection of bright dishes.

▲ **Half of this peninsula cabinetry is accessed** from the kitchen side and half from the dining room. A clever design trick was to borrow a few inches from the cabinet space to make shallow shelves custom-sized for a collection of snow globes, which make a cheery display for diners.

can make an impact on a room's looks while relieving storage problems.

However, there are a few things to consider when designing shelf storage. If items roll, for instance, shelves need a lip or some type of intermediate storage system, such as a basket or tray. This may seem obvious, but how many times has your mascara rolled off a shelf or out of a medicine cabinet? Have you ever cursed at a poorly designed lazy Susan? A high lip or curved back wall will keep pans or cans from flying out.

Shelf size also matters. When designing storage for frequently used items, consider closely spaced, shallow shelves; a perfect example is the pantry where all items should be easily seen and not stacked. The same holds true in the bathroom. Toiletries that are used every day should be easy to grab and replace. Long-term shelf storage can be

deeper, such as for boxes of holiday decorations, duffel bags of out-of-season sports gear, or backup packs of paper towels.

Hooks and pegs Hooks and pegs are ideal for hanging many items throughout the house, and you can't beat them for easy retrieval and return. Casual clothes, such as sweatshirts, fleece jackets, bathrobes, and hats, are perfect candidates for hooks. Hooks are also good for keeping dry towels at the ready near the shower or swimming pool, but they don't work for drying wet towels. Hooks are perfect for long, thin items with loops, and this covers a wide spectrum, from belts, ties, jewelry, and scarves (but only scarves that can be bunched) to dog leashes, aprons, and clipped-together mittens. Short, wide pegs attached close to the floor can make a

▲ A well-placed hook in this Arts and Crafts-inspired bathroom ensures that a bathrobe or towel is always in easy reach when exiting the shower.

great alternative form of shoe storage as proven in traditional Shaker closets. Think smaller hooks or pegs and you have storage solutions for any number of kitchen utensils and cookware. Think tiny hooks or clips and you have the classic method for hanging artwork and flat-backed sculpture, such as masks.

Rods For the most part, rods are used in closets or armoires to hold hangers, but they have other uses, too. Short, slender rods positioned ladder-style are perfect for scarves and ties, while larger rods in the laundry room—either attached to the wall or in the form of a drying rack—are ideal for the temporary storage of drying clothes and can even provide permanent storage for table linens. And, of course, rods are used as towel bars in the bath and kitchen. The fatter the rod, the more quickly a towel will dry; a double rod works even better.

▲ A Japanese alternative to drawers, the *tansu* is a highly adaptable, modular system of containers that are stacked together. This *tansu* not only provides a beautiful focal point but also substantial long- and short-term storage.

▲ This outdoor living space has an indoor-quality fireplace that features an elegant storage niche outfitted with two chunky wood shelves. The mantel-like topper creates an unexpected display space for an unusual pet.

Containers Containers can be a basket, box, trunk, or the most common household container of all: a drawer. Containers can hold things that roll (potatoes) or things that don't (sweaters), items that are flat (CDs and DVDs), or items that are bulky (pots). The most important thing to keep in mind when choosing a container is to match its size with the thing being contained so that there aren't too many layers to dig through. This means that a sock drawer will be reasonably shallow, as will a drawer for small kitchen tools, while a drawer for pots will be deep (and strong), as will a drawer for a fax machine.

Although drawers are built in, most containers are meant to be mobile. A noteworthy example is the stair-step *tansu* storage found in traditional Japanese homes. These modular storage systems comprise multiple boxes stacked on one another in such a way as to make a stair to an upper floor, while providing storage that can easily be relocated or even carried out in case of fire. While stair-step *tansu* boxes can't serve as stairs today (a no-no with building codes), they're a great example of container storage that is not only good looking but adaptable.

Slots, niches, and cubbyholes These scraps of storage space can be found in built-in or freestanding furniture, and even in walls themselves. They are really containers turned sideways, and are suited for flat or long, thin items, such as baking trays, rolling pins, pencils, envelopes, and wrapping paper. Commonly overlooked, these little bits of space can be the perfect solution for items that just don't work anywhere else.

Reconfigure, Replace, or Add On?

Storage can be improved by the smallest of changes or by the biggest of commitments, from the addition of a few shelves to the addition of an entire mudroom. You'll have to decide how much time, money, space, and thought you're willing to spend on storage improvements, but some is better than none, and even minute changes can have a worthwhile impact. An existing

▲**Take a couple of feet from the dining area, and you have a work space just off the kitchen.**
This work space allows homework to remain spread out during dinner, and it takes on the traditional role of being a spot to pay bills, make phone calls, and keep up with the family calendar.

home can become more efficient simply by adding a few off-the-shelf storage gadgets. Cabinets and closets can be reconfigured, and shelves can be added to leftover space. There may not be more square footage available for additional storage, but you're bound to find space somewhere that can be better designed.

Reconfigure Existing Storage

The least expensive, easiest way to improve storage—and one that doesn't require additional floor space—is to reconfigure existing storage space. Decide if items could be better stored in a different manner and install what's missing. Add narrow shelves, hooks, and racks to a bathroom, bedroom closet, or to the wall alongside the stair that runs between kitchen and basement. Add a rack for shoes or spices behind a door. Add a couple of shallow rows of shelves over a toilet. Add a peg rail next to the door. For inspiration and products, visit a home design store or shop online for storage accessories. Just be sure to measure everything and have a clear idea of what you need.

▶ **In the process of creating** a home for the TV, these homeowners gave their living room a whole new face and abundant storage. Using the coffered ceiling as a design cue, the built-in cabinetry is incorporated into the architecture, becoming the heart of this living room.

◀The space under a staircase can easily be claimed for storage. This closet is for sports gear and seasonal decorations.

▲The extra-wide cap on this window-height wainscoting makes an ideal track for a collection of model trains.

Replace Existing Storage with New

Need a bigger fix? It may be time to completely replace your current storage. Old kitchen cabinets that offer nothing but fixed shelves and minimal drawer space may be begging for retirement. New cabinets can be custom-designed to fit your exact needs, and there are so many off-the-shelf options these days that you can practically custom design cabinetry by selecting a variety of interchangeable units. Bedroom closets are notorious storage disasters, and if yours is a single-rod, single-shelf standard, it's a prime candidate for an upgrade.

Diversify limiting storage with an assortment of storage devices (there's a limitless array on the market), such as a stack of shelves, two shorter rods, and cubbies for shoes or accessories. And the living room could get a whole new lease on life if you toss the TV stand and invest in a real entertainment center with attached cabinetry and shelves for storing additional items, from videotapes to magazines to board games.

Claim Lost Space

If you have limited space, think like a designer of boats or space shuttles. Look around for free wall space or odd niches that can be claimed for storage; you'll be surprised how much dead space exists that can be perfect for squeezing in shelves, cubbies, or drawers. Look behind the knee walls in a top floor, over the door in the bathroom or bedroom, behind any door, or under a stair. The space under a bed can be claimed for large, rolling storage boxes, which can be a design feature built into the bed frame or cardboard concealed behind a dust ruffle.

Universal Accessibility

It may be advantageous to your present household or to a future situation to design universally accessible storage. The principles of universal design, which are specifically applied to design that works for those who are physically challenged or elderly, really makes good sense for everyone. Prime considerations in universal design include the ease of operation of hardware and the layout of furniture and built-in storage. For specifics about accessible design, check the Resources on p. 302; for a quick take, consider the following:

- The path from the door to where items are stored should be as short as possible, especially in a kitchen, which requires frequent restocking.
- Storage that is placed between 20 in. and 40 in. above the floor makes it easy for a sitting person to reach it.
- Fixed shelves are harder to access than pullout shelves or drawers, so they should be shallow.
- Fixed open shelves are much easier to access than fixed shelves behind closet doors.
- Full-extension drawer glides allow access to the entire drawer.
- Levers and wide wire pulls are much easier to use than knobs, especially ball-shaped knobs, which can be hard to grasp for everyone.
- A side-by-side refrigerator is easier to access than a fridge with the freezer at the top or bottom.
- Easy-to-switch or automatic lighting in closets—and even in cabinets— makes retrieving stored items a lot easier.

A dramatic example of this principle is a family that bought a house with a dumbwaiter, which was originally used for transporting food between the kitchen and lower-level dining area. Thinking it was too dangerous with three small children around, the homeowners disabled the cables and transformed the dumbwaiter box into a linen cupboard.

Add New Storage Areas

For the most serious storage puzzles, it may be worth the investment to add on a whole new storage area. An addition can be appended to the house or carved from existing space inside. Building a mudroom with an adjacent laundry and extra bathroom may be the perfect antidote to a family's entryway chaos, and a walk-in closet might be a better use of extra bedroom space than a huge bed and lots of furniture. A new pantry, media room, dressing room, or study may be the ticket to accommodate a growing family, hobby, or home-based business. Of course, the price tag will be higher than adding a shoe rack to the closet door, but the impact will be bigger, too.

◀▼ **This built-in cabinetry is positioned at the edge of a small** kitchen, where it provides space for dishware and for a small television that pulls out and can be swiveled for viewing from the kitchen island or an adjacent fireplace area. Mirrored doors conceal the television, along with a cabinet for videotapes, and reflect the rest of the kitchen, which adds depth to the space.

▲▶ **The standard bed-against-the-wall design has been** transformed into a bed that carries its own wall. The built-in headboard has a dual purpose of screening the bed from the dressing room and surrounding the bed with storage. Integral nightstands, bookshelves, and built-in lighting make the bed a comfortable place for quiet reading. The opposite side is both functional and elegant, with drawers for folded clothes and accessories, a shelf for temporary storage, and a huge mirror.

9

Entryway Storage

An efficient house—no matter how small—designates space for an entryway: a space for hanging up coats and hats, for stashing a wet umbrella, for taking off boots or sandy flip-flops. It has a place for plopping down the mail and grocery bags, and a row of hooks for backpacks and leashes—not to mention a spot for keys. And when space allows, it may even have an adjoining mudroom for life's messiest necessities. An ideal entryway is expressive as well, offering an introduction to the house's inhabitants. Umbrellas, boots, and backpacks coexist with more artful items, whether a beautiful flower arrangement, a collection of carved animals, a single painting, or an antique mirror.

A well-designed entryway helps organize a family's daily life, eliminating frantic morning searches for keys and shoes and briefcases. It creates a handy place for everything, so there's no tired parent in the evening telling the kids "one last time" to keep their skates out of the hallway. A fully appointed entryway also helps make you a more gracious, and less frantic, host with plenty of room to hang up coats, remove muddy shoes, and set down gifts. (I'm not counting those really big parties where a mountain of coats on the bed is a sure sign of hospitality.) In a nutshell, the ideal entryway helps you, and the house, exude both warmth and serenity.

▶This series of locker-like cubbies flanks the side entrance to a house with lots of kids. Each child has his or her own "locker" with adjustable shelves and rods that accommodate changing needs.

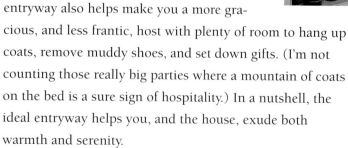

◀Without taking up much space, an antique display table lends charm to the entryway of this Mediterranean-farmhouse–style home, while providing the perfect temporary storage spot for keys, groceries, bills, or packages.

▲ **Coats and hats hung on a row of pegs** make an artful display in the entry hall of a rustic Martha's Vineyard cottage.

▲ **This small alcove off the** front door handles all sorts of storage, from kids' coats to everyone's shoes to groceries on their way to the kitchen. A window makes it feel more like a room than a closet.

So why are entryways often neglected? In part it's because people think that devoting their limited living space to an entryway is frivolous. But even the smallest Inuit igloo—much smaller than even a modest frame house—provides an entry hall with a bump-out storage vault for clothing and harnesses. The Inuit aren't the only ones with winter coats and dog leashes, so if they can spare the room, so can we. Even in a small house, carving out a bit of room to better organize inbound and outbound traffic (and all the stuff that goes along for the ride) is space well spent, because it eliminates clutter in the rest of the house for more functional and comfortable living.

A Welcoming Entry

An entryway acts as the launch pad for the day's activities and as a temporary receptacle for the paraphernalia your family accumulates during the day. That word "temporary" is key to a working entryway: You need space that can handle grocery bags, mail, and backpacks while you kick off boots and take off coats but not make it easy to keep things there for any length of time. This is where you designate a spot for outbound mail and park backpacks after homework is done; create some easy-access flat space for all the random stuff of life—on a hall desk, on a cantilevered shelf, in a niche carved into a thick wall, on extended stair treads that are bench-high; and a space for outgoing library books and clothes for the cleaners.

▲ **The bookcase/display** surface is kept low in this entry hall so as not to detract from the view, but it still provides ample storage.

▶ **In this small house, the** entryway is delineated not by walls but by a blue-tiled inglenook with a fireplace and built-in bench, perfect for removing boots or storing backpacks, library books, and other things coming and going. A very modest coat closet just fits in on the left.

►**This tiled foyer is actually** the second step in a gracious transition from entrance deck to living spaces (see the drawing below). Niches provide display storage, while the slatted door leads to a generous coat closet that handles the majority of utilitarian storage.

The Front Entrance

Those of us who come home through the front door need a place to accommodate gear without downgrading the atmosphere; first impressions are more important here than at the back door, calling for finer finishes and less utilitarian storage spots. It may suit your style to simply line the entryway with a Shaker-style peg rail and a narrow shelf for hats and gloves, or you may prefer a more elaborate scheme. It doesn't matter as long as it suits your lifestyle and there's a place for all essential items.

In large houses of yore, the front door opened onto the front hall, which is still a fine tradition if you have the space. A front hall is useful because it acts as a transition space between public and private areas, as well as providing space for built-in closets, freestanding storage furniture, and the simplest of storage amenities—hooks, pegs, and shelves. Even if your house has limited space, try to create an area that is screened off from the living space in some way, by a panel of stained glass, for example, or by a partial wall or a bookcase.

A Small Addition with Big Potential

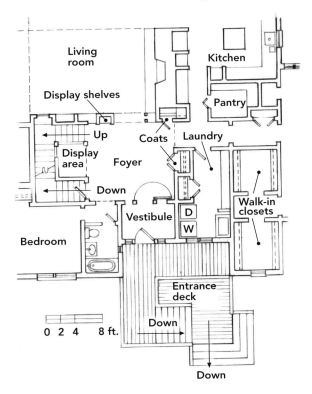

◀**Simple and elegant, this back-door** birch-veneer plywood unit keeps contents accessible. Kids claim the lower two cubbies, while parents keep their gear in the top sections. A wall outlet is a smart detail, allowing the cell phone to charge, ready to grab on the way out.

◀**This lovely back entry hall**, complete with warm, natural light, ample hooks for coats, a hall bench for shoe changing, and even a sleeping dog, welcomes a family home just as graciously as a front door.

Storage with an Eye on History

To maintain an authentic period look in an old house, handle entryway storage with freestanding furniture like coat racks, armoires, cabinets, and hall benches. To make a built-in closet look like an armoire or cupboard, stop it short of the ceiling and trim it with molding; detail the base trim with legs, much like a traditional-style kitchen cabinet. Or, for a more minimalist version, take a cue from the Shakers, who built cloakrooms that were lined with pegs—just above eye level for coats and close to the floor for shoes and boots. These cloakrooms accommodated the outerwear of many people, but in these not-so-simple times, a family of four could easily fill such a space.

The Back Entrance

If the front door is used only by guests and delivery people, focus your energy on the back door and make it as functional and appealing as you would a front entrance—the family entrance should be just as welcoming as the guest entrance. It may not be as formal a space, but the back entrance will still benefit from thoughtful design; the same storage principles apply, but the storage units can be a little more relaxed to suit the space and your family's habits. Regardless of how formal or casual, the back door will be a more welcoming entrance if it's not a minefield of shoes, pet bowls, and recycling bins. As is discussed later in this chapter, back entrances can also be given a major boost from adjoining mudrooms, the MVPs of modern life.

► **A built-in seat between** white oak cabinets separates this entryway from the dining area. Two coat closets are situated in the wall behind the cabinets, providing extra storage without cluttering this elegant space.

The Hall Closet

Whether you call it a coat closet or a hall closet, a 2-ft.-deep space to hang up coats may seem prosaic, but just try living without one. Clothes trees and hat stands can work for the very tidy, but they're not for everyone, especially not active children. Clothes trees also take up a lot of room, particularly during the cold months when layers of coats seem to mushroom uncontrollably. Hooks are great for unstructured outerwear, such as sweatshirts and kids' jackets, but a dress coat or jacket shouldn't spend more than an evening on a hook. Hangers are the answer for better outerwear, and a closet also provides shelves for hats and other accessories, along with a space for shoes.

A front hall closet can find a doubly useful life if it's treated as a piece of the architecture. Instead of building a closet into the wall, build it as a box that divides entry and living spaces. Extend the box to the ceiling to make a more substantial, thick wall between areas, or, for more free-flowing light and views, stop the closet short of the ceiling. Building a closet within the house rather than at the perimeter also frees up the walls for windows.

Make the Most of a Small Coat Closet

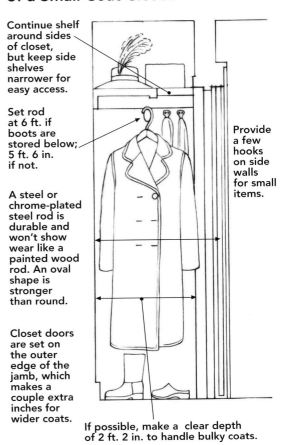

Continue shelf around sides of closet, but keep side shelves narrower for easy access.

Set rod at 6 ft. if boots are stored below; 5 ft. 6 in. if not.

A steel or chrome-plated steel rod is durable and won't show wear like a painted wood rod. An oval shape is stronger than round.

Closet doors are set on the outer edge of the jamb, which makes a couple extra inches for wider coats.

Provide a few hooks on side walls for small items.

If possible, make a clear depth of 2 ft. 2 in. to handle bulky coats.

◀One stair tread is stretched around the corner to make a welcoming bench in a Normandy-style cottage. A door in the bench opens to reveal storage space for coats and blankets.

▲A big family requires a lot of bench room when they all pile in after skating or swimming, and a large U-shaped bench is the perfect answer. The fastest way to hang up a coat is on pegs, so there are plenty here.

A Deeper Closet

While it's generally true that the most convenient storage space is one-item deep, the front hall closet can break that rule. If you have limited wall space but adequate depth, adopt a design detail from early 20th-century New York City apartments and make a double deep closet. Use the inner rod for out-of-season coats and clothes.

Have a Seat

The most welcoming entryway will offer not only a place to hang your hat but also a place to sit and deal with shoes, wait for slower siblings, or read the mail. While an entryway's size will dictate how elaborate the seating is, a well-designed entryway should offer something to sit on. The seat can be a simple, open bench—perfect for stashing boots beneath—or a luxurious built-in storage trunk with padded seat. Or, keep your eyes open for an antique or reproduction hall bench; this handsome piece of furniture can be found in styles ranging from simple country pine models to extravagant Arts and Crafts pieces with mirrors, umbrella racks, benches, boot shelves, and forests of hooks.

Fifty Square Feet Make a Whole New House

◀Outside, stone steps and sidewalls, along with a bracketed gable roof, make a generous, welcoming, and rainproof entry porch.

▼A hall bench with hidden storage and hooks bordering the mirror adds charm as well as service to this small but functional addition. A new coat closet is on the left.

When Massachusetts architect Lynn Hopkins bought a small Cape with her husband, their house had a front door that opened smack dab into the living room, offering no place to stash wet boots and hang coats, much less a hat. In addition, the entry stoop had no protection from rain. The family's daily lives got an instant makeover with the addition of a mere 50 sq. ft. of indoor space, plus a generous porch protected by a gabled overhang.

But the addition wasn't just plunked in front of the existing front door. Instead, Lynn moved the front door 7 ft. to the side to keep traffic from marching through the center of the living room. She then added a vestibule complete with a coat closet on one side and a handsome hall bench, which her father made, on the other; a weather-proof (and very easy to clean) bluestone floor completes this well-designed solution to a big storage problem.

Finally, there's a place to store wet boots, snowy coats, and discarded backpacks, along with a seating area that can serve a number of purposes, from shoe-changing station to prop for a basket of Halloween candy.

Stairway Storage

Many entryways, whether at the front or back of the house, have a stairway that can provide an often underused—not to mention misused—storage area. It's tempting to set items bound for the upstairs or outdoors on the staircase, but this is a messy and potentially dangerous habit. Instead, design stair treads that extend past the balustrade, which will provide a safer but just as accessible storage area and do double duty as informal seating. Another way to increase stair storage is to forgo an open balustrade and extend side walls to railing height; expand the walls to make a staging area for display pieces, or designate it as an unexpected nook to sit in and read.

▶**This wide, stepped railing** offers ample space for display (and cats). Doors on the other side of the staircase, which face the living room, make good use of the dead space within the railing.

◀A Craftsman-style stair-
case, built of walnut, Douglas
fir, and eucalyptus, features
stair-stepped doors along
the side that are fitted with
leaded-glass panels. Storage
under the stairs handles
boots, coats, and other
seasonal items.

▲This entryway bookshelf, recessed into
the staircase and well lit by a window in the
hip-roof dormer, serves as storage space for
books, CDs, art objects, and outgoing mail.

Looking beyond the stairs themselves, the staircase can
provide additional storage room underneath. Although there
seems to be a lot of dead space under a staircase, much of it
is consumed by the stair structure. Depending on the design
of the stair, it may be possible to create interesting storage
niches, or even built-in boxes or drawers. It is important to
remember, however, that stairs are your main egress from
upper floors in the event of a fire, so flammable material—
paint cans, paper goods—shouldn't be stored under them.
Good candidates for under-stair storage are out-of-season
woolens, footwear, and sporting gear. In a multifamily building, the local building codes should be checked before
putting anything under a staircase.

The Mudroom

In a suburban or rural house, a mudroom—or even a mud corner—is a necessity. This is the down-and-dirty way to enter the house without damaging finer finishes, and it deserves to be mandatory for any climate that has recurring rain or snow in the forecast. A mudroom may not be the prettiest part of the house, but it works hard and should get as much attention as the rest of your home. No one ever regrets making space for a mudroom.

While an essential element to consider in the design of a new house, the mudroom is also worth making room for in an existing house. Situate this space where it can best catch family members and guests with wet or dirty shoes, snowy layers, dripping bathing suits, or sweaty sporting gear. If building a mudroom isn't an option, carve out a section of the kitchen, or a hallway near the kitchen, if possible, or claim a chunk of the garage to enclose and outfit as a mudroom. Actually, the mudroom can be near the back door, the front door, or the only door. If the mudroom is near the front (or only) door, however, gentrify the space or situate it off to the side, which will help contain the dirt and dampness.

▲ A formal entry and mudroom are rolled into one in this coastal Massachusetts house for a large, young family. The tall entry space is ringed with windows and anchored by a 3-ft. diagonal bench that's divided into quadrants for shoe storage, with additional storage for shoes and outerwear in a doorless niche to the side. Opposite (see floor plan) is a coat closet with pegs, hangers, and shelves.

An Entry and Mudroom in One

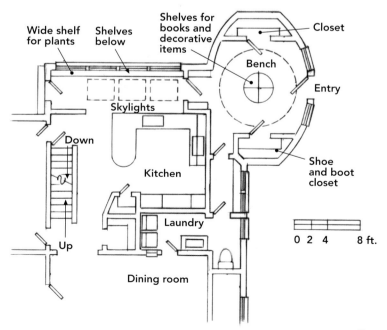

Wide shelf for plants
Shelves below
Shelves for books and decorative items
Closet
Bench
Entry
Skylights
Down
Kitchen
Shoe and boot closet
Laundry
0 2 4   8 ft.
Up
Dining room

▲ **This spacious, welcoming** entry hall has a tough, handsome slate floor and built-in, locker-style cabinets that flank a long bench for changing shoes. The large window lights not only illuminate the entry hall but also the living room beyond.

Make Room for Pets

Consider amenities for the family pets when you design a mudroom—it can double as a perfect haven for them, provided the room temperature is stable. Reserve a basket for drying pet towels and toys, and save a few hooks for leashes. A protected corner is ideal for food dishes, and another corner might make the perfect place for a dog or cat bed. A pet door could be just the thing for an independent dog with a fenced yard.

◀▼A stack of large cubbyholes flanks this door, creating handy space to stash boots and shoes. Off to the right are hooks and a bench to accommodate shoe changing and outerwear.

Sizing Up Mudroom Cabinetry

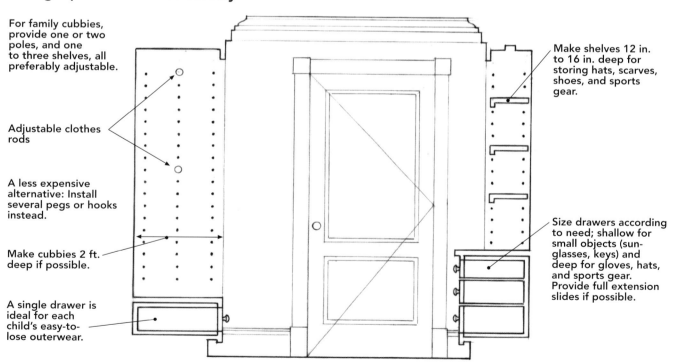

For family cubbies, provide one or two poles, and one to three shelves, all preferably adjustable.

Adjustable clothes rods

A less expensive alternative: Install several pegs or hooks instead.

Make cubbies 2 ft. deep if possible.

A single drawer is ideal for each child's easy-to-lose outerwear.

Make shelves 12 in. to 16 in. deep for storing hats, scarves, shoes, and sports gear.

Size drawers according to need; shallow for small objects (sunglasses, keys) and deep for gloves, hats, and sports gear. Provide full extension slides if possible.

A Mudroom Built for Kids

Active kids don't have to be high maintenance if there's a place for all their gear. This bright mudroom addition has it all, starting with accessibility. There's a "front" door from the driveway, which opens onto a bench, and there's a back door that opens onto the backyard. The built-in bench opens to reveal space for storing big stuff, and a bank of face-frame cabinetry with inset drawers and door—and with ample cubbies—holds everything from swimsuits to crayons. A traditional peg rail with shelf makes it easy for the three children to hang up coats and backpacks and keeps hats, sports gear, and gloves off the floor.

The cabinetry is kept at a 3-ft. height so that a band of windows can brighten up the space, which often becomes a playroom, even though there's a family room nearby. The countertop provides more storage space for outdoor gear and plants, but it's also a handy spot for preparing mail for the outgoing mailbox, opening mail, reading the paper, and enjoying a distant view of Long Island Sound. To ensure that this is no mere passageway, hinged frames above the window provide rotating gallery space for kid art.

▶ **Each section of this** built-in bench makes a separate, lightweight lid, making it a much safer storage space for kids' toys and gear. Because this mudroom is so pleasant, this bench is more than a space to take off boots— it makes a wonderful window seat for reading.

◀**There's no better way** to encourage kids to keep an entryway neat than to provide them with pegs and a shelf, making it a one-stroke action to hang up a coat or backpack.

▼**Shallow drawers are great** for mittens, hats, and small sports gear, such as goggles and jump ropes. Open cubbies are a perfect solution for beach towels, swimsuits, and flip-flop storage.

A Two-Stage Mudroom for an Active Family

Inhabited by a family that loves the outdoors, this house has a bilevel side entry that tackles storage in two stages. The lower-level mudroom handles messier storage with an easy-to-clean tile floor and a bench for removing and storing muddy or wet boots. The closed-door cabinetry has shelves and rods for outerwear storage, while numerous hooks suspend a burgeoning collection of baseball caps.

The lighter color scheme in the entry hall, which is three steps up, signals a transition to the more formal living area, but it, too, provides an abundance of practical storage. Individual lockers hold additional sporting gear and outerwear for each family member, along with high-priority items like keys, backpacks, and even outgoing bills. With everything stored together in a well-designed and dedicated spot, the family's comings and goings are smooth and stress-free.

▲ **This room is the first step in a double-barreled** entryway, with space for storing boots below the cantilevered cabinetry. A sunroom beyond the windows exchanges light with the mudroom, depending on the time of day.

▲ **It would have been simpler to just build a** full-height closet with double doors, but designing entryway storage as frame-and-panel cabinetry is an elegant touch in a barrel-vaulted hall. Separate doors and shelves keep each child's gear and outerwear untangled from the others'.

Untangle Sporting Gear

A mudroom is the perfect place to store sports gear. If you designate a specific place, there's a chance your daughter will actually put her lacrosse stick there instead of taking it upstairs to practice against her bedroom wall. Dumping everything into one large box, however, won't do the trick. Check out home-improvement stores and catalogs for racks that hang over the door or on the wall and that will hold several large balls and a few bats, gloves, and sticks (see Resources on p. 302). If you can afford the space, sports lockers (one per family member is a luxury—or a necessity) are a perfect storage solution, and if you're handy, you can build your own fairly easily. All you need now is a shower room.

▲A modest-sized mudroom off the back door of a country house is endowed with a lovely and highly functional laundry (washer and dryer are on the opposite wall), including a vitreous-china farmhouse sink with a drying rack overhead and open shelves for linens. Cabinets below hold cleaning supplies and wide pulls double as towel bars. Wide, tall cubbies handle laundry baskets.

A Well-Placed Laundry Room

A laundry room is the natural partner of a mudroom. If you have the space, position the washer and dryer near—or even in—the mudroom. Gardeners, sports enthusiasts, and families with children and pets will all make good use of a large, utilitarian sink in this area, as well as rods for hanging dripping clothes. An adjacent bathroom is a godsend for children (and their parents), whose need for such a facility seems to increase exponentially with their exposure to snowsuits and lawn sprinklers. Finally, to make this space the most valuable in the house, locate recycling bins here, and make it the mandatory route for taking out compost and trash.

10

Kitchen Storage

▶**A stretch of open shelving** in this kitchen provides display and storage while balancing long expanses of closed cabinetry.

A kitchen is prime real estate. It has the most expensive square footage of any room in the house, and it's the place everyone wants to be. A kitchen is also the repository for the widest variety of items in the house, making it a likely source of chaos unless its storage space is well thought out. Cookie-cutter cabinetry—wall cabinet over base cabinet, drawer over door—is all too often the only space allocated for storage, and it never seems to provide enough room for everything. Pots and pans end up in a jumbled heap, while fine china and everyday dishes make dangerous bedfellows in overcrowded cabinets. Utensils tangle and jam shallow drawers, and there's no room to prepare dinner because the counters are strewn with clutter that doesn't have a permanent home. But kitchen storage doesn't have to be an accident waiting to happen.

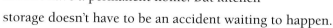

◀**This architectural gem, hewn from wood and stone, incorporates a wide range of storage** possibilities that complement one another in both practical and aesthetic terms. The built-in piece in the middle of the room acts as a kitchen island on one side and a wet bar on the other. A combination of closed and open cabinetry creates visual interest, as well as storage space that's conducive to all manner of kitchen gear.

◀**Thanks to a smart remodel, this tiny** kitchen—100 sq. ft.—has become fully functional. A range used to be where the dishwasher now is; moving it to a bare wall allowed for an additional 2 ft. of counter space and lots of extra storage above. Drawers contain small tools and supplies, a lazy Susan stores pots and pans, and pullouts under the sink hold garbage and recycling.

For one thing, cabinetry can be built to handle specific needs. Base cabinets can be outfitted with drawers instead of doors if it better suits your needs, and wall cabinets can be designed with open shelves. Or forgo a few cabinets and attach shelves directly to the wall for extra-easy access. Dishes, particularly the formal variety, may be better off in freestanding furniture, such as an armoire or hutch. And pantries are reemerging as a modern necessity as more households buy in bulk. You'll find all these storage options in this chapter, as well as suggestions for storing specific items—the equipment and tools you need for cooking, cold foods and dry goods, spices, wine, cookbooks, and more prosaic items, including garbage and cleaning supplies. And since the kitchen has become more than just a place to pre-pare meals, you'll find ways to make space for a desk and its accessories, for children to work and play, and for the dis-play of more artful items.

Storage Options

Your personal style will dictate how you designate storage space in the kitchen. If you lean toward modern design, select sleek cabinets, streamlined shelves, and unfussy hardware. If you prefer more traditional elements, you might choose a Craftsman-style kitchen that features wooden cabinets in concert with built-in benches and shelves. Aficionados of restaurant-style kitchens might store much of their kitchen gear and nonperishable food out in the open on stainless-steel wire racks and open shelving.

The way you use your kitchen will also influence how you create storage. Do you prefer a compact space for cooking with an adjacent (but out-of-the-way) spot for kids doing homework or guests keeping the cook company? Or is the kitchen a large, common room designed to accommodate multiple, simultaneous activities?

The storage needs of these kitchens will be different, but regardless of personal style and kitchen habits, you'll benefit

▲ ◀There's plenty of room for storage in this Martha's Vineyard kitchen without resorting to wall cabinets, which would block the captivating views. Tall base cabinets with a drawer over each, corner storage shelves, and a pot rack all meet specific storage needs. The arrangement allows for a pass-through to the dining/living space, which supplies additional work and storage space.

from creating a range of storage options. A selection of cabinetry, open shelving, and pantry storage ensures not only a handsome kitchen, but also one that operates smoothly. If you balance three walls of cabinets with a generous opening into a family room, or contrast closed cabinets with open storage, your kitchen will feel more open and more serene. Functionality can (and should) coexist with aesthetics, which will make time spent in the kitchen more productive and more pleasurable.

▲ **A wall of frameless maple** cabinets with flush overlay flat-panel doors and drawers is a striking feature in this contemporary house. The tall cabinet in the corner of the kitchen is a pantry. To keep up with an active entertaining schedule, the homeowners installed an under-counter refrigerator for beverages and cocktail fixings.

◀A kitchen with a high, gabled ceiling makes it possible to enjoy the view yet still have room for wall cabinets. Glass backs to the cabinets would have brightened the kitchen even more but also would have required more frequent and fastidious cleaning.

▲Two walls of crisp, white, painted cabinets with flush overlay doors and drawers are punctuated by a collection of fixed and operable windows, as well as glass display shelves (shelves are lit by halogens at night). The upper row of wall cabinets overhangs the lower wall cabinets by ¾ in.

◀No wall cabinets here: These are hung from the ceiling, allowing light from the huge kitchen windows to bounce into the breakfast nook. Frameless base cabinets are supported on stainless-steel legs rather than being anchored to the floor—a purposefully light and modern detail.

A Harmonious Mix of Texture, Color, and Shape

It's hard to imagine that this bright, beautiful, family kitchen was once dark and cramped. Seattle architect Geoff Prentiss took on the task of evoking a Tuscan farmhouse, creating a kitchen that is both eclectic and unified. The storage changes from floor to ceiling, with each horizontal layer creating a different level of openness; from closed cabinets and open shelves to semitransparent storage in the form of

baskets and frosted-glass doors, this kitchen has a little bit of everything.

Prentiss made the kitchen rich in history and variety by using a restored cast-iron sink and terra-cotta coping pieces (rescued from a demolished Seattle building), which make hefty, stylish shelves over the massive French range. Despite the mix of color, texture, and shape, the kitchen feels placid, thanks to a deliberate use of symmetry

▲**Thanks to a breathtaking variety of materials** and types of storage in this kitchen, there is no sign of clutter, as much of the storage is hidden in drawers and behind frosted glass doors. The few open shelves on this side of the kitchen display objects both pleasing and useful.

▲**Reclaimed terra-cotta coping pieces create** appropriate shelves for a few traditional kitchen tools, such as a mortar and pestle and an Italian oil cruet.

◄The aspen branches that appear to hold up shelves, countertops, and even the island cabinets actually have their cores drilled out and are slid over supporting cables or rods.

▲ Although each of these drawer pulls is different, all are wrought iron and of similar heft. Even the refrigerator door has been fitted with a custom wrought-iron handle (the freezer drawer opens by a built-in, full-width pull).

and repetition, and a mellow palette of colors that are earthy and warm. Each wall contains symmetry of some kind—shelves and cabinets flank the sink and range, and drawers are aligned with like materials in rows. Around the perimeter, maple, flat-panel drawers anchor the base cabinets, while the upper portion is left open and filled with baskets. Other materials are repeated throughout the kitchen, such as the toekicks, drawer fronts, and range hood, all of which are prerusted and then sealed steel. Almost all of the base cabinet storage is provided by drawers of varying sizes crafted in a variety of materials, providing versatile storage for a range of items, from pots and pans to dish towels.

Eclectic Storage in a Cozy Kitchen

When the owner of this kitchen asked architect Tom Vermeland for a "simple house that doesn't look designed," he complied by creating the essence of an old English cottage, mixing built-ins and free-standing furniture, and using a variety of colors and textures. There are no standard wall cabinets in this kitchen; instead, storage is handled with more old-fashioned solutions like open, fixed shelves, an armoire for dishes, and a built-in cabinet that extends all the way to the countertop as if it were a hutch. A walk-in pantry, an invaluable detail in many old houses, also helps make up for lost cabinet space. The arched niche (complete with ventilation), where a restored 1930s range holds court, also gives the sense of a kitchen from a different time. The overall effect is one of charm, comfort, serenity, and—as the client wished—a sense of design with a small "d."

▲ **Storage comes from many sources in this** comfortable kitchen. An armoire conveniently houses fine china near the dining table, and base cabinets with drawers handle pots, pans, and small tools. A floor-to-countertop cabinet has additional storage, while everyday dishes are displayed on open, fixed shelves near the dishwasher. Open shelves for cookbooks face a sitting area.

▲ **The 1930s range was salvaged from a relative's basement,** restored, and installed in a ventilated cooking niche. Storage for a few pans and small cooking tools is supplied by a small table and two fixed shelves.

Basic Cabinet Types

FRAMELESS CABINET

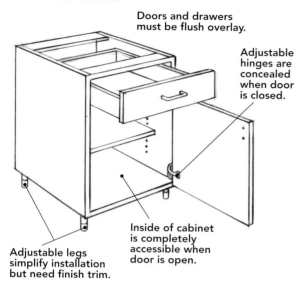

Doors and drawers must be flush overlay.

Adjustable hinges are concealed when door is closed.

Adjustable legs simplify installation but need finish trim.

Inside of cabinet is completely accessible when door is open.

FACE-FRAME CABINET

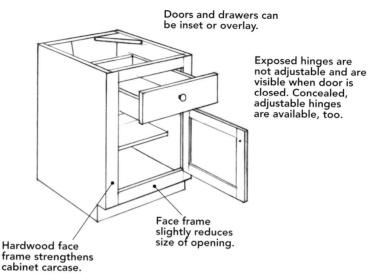

Doors and drawers can be inset or overlay.

Exposed hinges are not adjustable and are visible when door is closed. Concealed, adjustable hinges are available, too.

Face frame slightly reduces size of opening.

Hardwood face frame strengthens cabinet carcase.

▲ **Traditional frame-and-panel, solid cherry** doors open to a plastic-laminate interior that's bright and easy to clean. Edges are banded with cherry to match the doors.

Cabinet Basics

By far, cabinetry is still the most common and versatile type of kitchen storage, and it's also the most expensive. Whether you're remodeling or starting from scratch, there are seemingly endless cabinetry options, which can be overwhelming. Start by following your first impressions. Even if you don't know the terminology, you probably already have a preference for face-frame rather than frameless cabinets and inset doors rather than overlay doors, or vice versa. But knowing how to ask for what you want will ensure that you get it.

Face-frame cabinets are traditionally American and are still the most popular cabinet style manufactured. A solid-wood frame is attached to the case, and doors either overlay the frame or are inset flush with the frame (more expensive because it's more precise). The European-born frameless cabinet gets its strength from a thicker case and requires no stiffening face frame. Because the case itself has thin edges, doors and drawers overlap so that they almost touch. Frameless cabinets have long been associated with sleek modern styles, but today's frameless cabinets can look completely traditional with panels and molding. Both cabinet types can be fitted with adjustable concealed hinges, but for

◀ **This kitchen features a clever and diverse use of space,**
with an assortment of closed cabinets, small drawers for tools,
a cupboard for small appliances, a glazed cabinet for dishes, and
open shelves for books.

▲ **This kitchen has an agreeable balance of**
open shelving and closed cabinets, and there's
even a middle ground with screened panels on
base cabinet doors. Rather than fill the wall over
the sink with cabinets, it is opened to create a
connection with the family room.

true period-style cabinets, a face-frame cabinet with inset
doors and butt hinges should be selected. What's the difference as far as storage goes? For the same-size box, face-
frame cabinets have a little less room because the projecting
frame makes it more difficult to fit items snugly in a cabinet,
and the drawers must be somewhat smaller to fit within the
face frame. Otherwise, the differences are largely stylistic.

Cabinet style affects drawer storage, too. Traditional
drawers open by gliding on wooden slides, and a few cabinetmakers still make them that way, but the majority of drawers
are fitted with steel slides and nylon rollers or ball bearings,
which are more durable and stable. If you're purchasing high-
end drawers with elegant details, such as dovetails, you
might not appreciate side-mounted drawer slides detracting
from the aesthetics when the drawer is open. Under-
mounted drawer slides are another option. They're more
expensive than side-mounted slides, and they reduce the

▲**These custom cabinets feature tin renderings** that create a front panel for the cabinet doors, proving that the sky's the limit when it comes to custom design. The cabinets stop just shy of the beadboard ceiling to make room for a display of cast-iron pots and ceramic bowls.

▲**Adjacent cabinets definitely don't need to** match, and these custom cabinets were created to complement each other's patterns, colors, and styles. Because they were made to order according to the homeowner's whimsical vision, they are one-of-a-kind and perfectly suited to this kitchen's specific storage needs.

depth of available drawer space, but they allow for more width because the slides don't eat up space on the drawer sides. Under-mount slides can handle a lot of weight but expect to pay more than for side mounts with the same capacity—and check manufacturer specifications before planning to use under-mount slides on a large pot drawer.

Cabinet sources Deciding where to buy your cabinets can be just as daunting as choosing a style. These days, there's a huge range of products, from do-it-yourself to custom-made, and everything in between, with an equally vast range of prices. Skilled homeowners may enjoy the challenge and cost savings of knocked-down (KD) or ready-to-assemble (RTA) cabinets. Look for KD cabinets at retailers like Ikea; RTA components are often sold exclusively to contractors or cabinetmakers, but it's worth investigating. These cabinets allow you to mix and match hardware, styles, and colors, but they also require patience, precision, and a willingness to be responsible for installation.

Stock cabinets come in standard sizes and finishes; they're generally the most affordable option (if you're not doing it yourself) and are available off the shelf or within a few weeks. Semicustom and custom cabinets offer a much more extensive selection of styles, finishes, and sizes than

Island Storage

The kitchen island has been around for centuries, but in most cases, solely as a work space. Today's smarter islands harbor a wealth of storage whether in cabinets, shelves, or on hooks and bars. Even if people will be sitting at the island, it can still accommodate storage; cabinets or shelf units can be installed on opposite ends with open space in the middle. If storage takes priority, the entire island can be filled with cabinetry.

An island countertop provides its own wealth of storage space, but it can easily become cluttered and useless for food preparation if it turns into a dumping ground for mail, cookbooks, and other shelf litter—make sure that kind of storage has a designated spot elsewhere.

When selecting an island, keep in mind that freestanding islands are more flexible, but you'll need a built-in if you want to incorporate electrical outlets. An island with wheels is a good choice for kitchens with multiple cooks.

▲An old chest is given new life as a kitchen island. The unit provides pot and pan storage that's partially obscured by screened panels.

▲Cooking in this kitchen is made easy by ample storage in open shelves and wide, deep drawers. The filigreed island has multiple functions, providing a work space, storage space, and a serving counter.

The Inside Scoop on Wood Cabinetry

We say we have wood cabinets, and we're right in a way, but cabinets are rarely made from solid wood, except for the frames and doors of custom face-frame cabinetry. Most components are actually made from panels, also called sheet goods or engineered wood, either of which may receive a veneer of wood.

Sheet goods are manufactured from wood, wood by-products, and even nonwood sources. The most common are plywood, medium-density fiberboard (MDF), and particleboard. Plywood is stronger and lighter than MDF and particleboard, it's easier to curve, and it holds screws better. But it's also more expensive and not as smooth, making the veneer application more difficult.

A recent development, combined-core plywood, utilizes the best qualities of sheet goods by sandwiching plywood between layers of MDF or particleboard. The result is a smoother, lighter panel that holds screws well. Don't think of engineered wood as a lesser cousin of wood, however, because overall, it's actually more dimensionally stable than solid wood.

▲ **A wide, deep drawer next to a butcher-block work space provides** ample room for a salad spinner, storage containers, and work bowls.

◀**Drawer details differ** according to the size of the drawer. Shallow drawers have flush flat panels while deeper drawers can handle a panel with molding. One recessed panel keeps dish towels out of the way but within reach of the cook.

stock cabinets, and, not surprisingly, they also cost quite a bit more. But if you have very specific ideas about what you want or if you have an unusually configured kitchen, custom cabinets can be designed to your exact specifications. Depending on how customized your cabinets are, it can take 6 to 20 weeks for delivery.

Drawers versus doors In the 1950s, Cornell University conducted a landmark kitchen study, but it took half a century for consumers to embrace one of its primary findings—that the more drawers the merrier in the kitchen.

◀An almost all-drawer kitchen contains a combination of narrow, wide, shallow, and deep drawers. The large drawer under the cooktop provides the perfect storage place for pots and pans.

▲▲A hybrid of shelf and drawer, this sliding shelf offers convenient access to pots and pans while keeping them tidy and contained behind a door.

For years, the cabinetry standard was one medium-sized drawer over a base cabinet with fixed shelves and one or two doors. This design still works for some people, but many of today's kitchens are justifiably drawer happy.

Increasingly, drawers are replacing shelving in base cabinets, which makes great design sense in many cases; instead of rummaging through a dark cabinet on your hands and knees for the pasta boiler, you can simply pull open the pot and pan drawer. Drawers closest to the countertop are often the most shallow, while subsequent drawers are deeper, but that isn't a hard-and-fast rule. They can be designed in any dimensions that suit your needs. A deeper top drawer is perfect for boxes of wrap and foil, smaller tools, or that "useful" stuff everyone seems to collect. Super-deep drawers should be reserved for the big stuff, such as pots and pans; a 10-in.-deep drawer packed to the brim with utensils will prove futile—if not downright maddening.

Corner cabinets Corner cabinets can be a curse or a blessing. They offer a respectable amount of extra storage space, but if they're not set up with care, they're rendered useless, not to mention annoying. Cabinet manufacturers offer a number of accessories to help consumers better utilize this space, including lazy Susans and pullout racks of varying complexity. Lazy Susans can be the perfect solution, but not if items come flying off every time the unit is spun around; some have a high rim, or, even better, a curved backing, both of which will help keep items in place. If you don't need the extra cabinet storage, forgo corner base cupboards altogether and make the space an open garage for a rolling garbage pail or a step-ladder. For corner wall storage, open shelving is a great alternative to closed cabinetry; in addition to offering easier access, the shelves will open up the kitchen and provide an eye-pleasing counterpoint to closed cabinetry.

▲**An unusual corner drawer makes good** use of a usually wasted space. Base cabinet storage is handled by fixed shelves and a piano-hinged door.

▶**Lazy Susans rank high on the list** for making use of corner cabinet storage. If the corner is not close to an appliance, there's room to hang two doors that meet at the corner when they close as shown here. If there's limited clearance, the doors can be joined by a piano hinge.

Cabinet hardware Cabinet hardware can greatly influence a kitchen's looks—and its budget. Like cabinets, hardware runs the gamut in costs, styles, and availability. Pulls are the stars of cabinet hardware, and they come in an endless array of designs, from popular bin pulls to wire pulls to knobs and latches. Wire pulls won't snag clothing, they're easier to grasp than knobs, and, if they're long enough, they can double as towel bars. On the other hand, knobs are easier to replace if a kitchen is being remodeled.

Hinges aren't as obvious as pulls, but they shouldn't be neglected either. Concealed adjustable hinges (developed for frameless cabinets but now made for face-frame cabinets, too) allow for easier installation and adjustment than butt hinges. Butt hinges, however, are still the more authentic option for a period kitchen, and they're also less obvious than adjustable hinges in glass cabinetry.

▲**Cabinets with full-overlay** doors are fitted with long stainless-steel handles, handy for hanging dish towels. Drawers of varying depths provide versatile storage. Note the knife storage built into the granite ledge over the sink.

► **Thin, white shelves display scores of** cookbooks in a casual dining room, along with antique kitchen tools, including stoneware jugs and a mortar and pestle.

▲ **A built-in hutch provides storage space** for linens and seldom-used serving pieces in the closed cabinets below; a dishware collection is stored and displayed on the open shelves above.

Open Shelves

In addition to drawers, the Cornell kitchen study applauded open shelves, especially those positioned at eye level and just above and below. Open shelving hung over food preparation areas gives you more room to work than bulky, low-hanging cabinets (or cluttered counters), as well as a greater sense of openness. And shelves are ideal for storing a whole host of items, from dishes to stockpots to spices. It's important to match the function of the shelf with the design of the shelf, considering size, method of support, material, and finish. While you can store almost anything on a shelf as long as it's structurally up to the task, location should, to a certain extent, dictate shelf size. A good rule of thumb is to keep shelves at head level more narrow than higher shelves and to use them for smaller items, like spices, that only require a few inches to perch on.

Shelves can be as narrow as 2 in. or as wide as 2 ft., but here are some standard guidelines: Allow 8 in. minimum for cookbook shelves, 12 in. to 15 in. for dishware, and 18 in. or wider for pots and pans. Spacing shelves can be tricky. If you space shelves far apart, you'll be tempted to stack dishes and glasses too high. Better to use more shelves spaced closer together, which makes it safer and easier to access dishes—and everything else, for that matter. Should shelving be adjustable? That's an individual decision, but think about this: If shelving is designed to fit the items you normally store, and if it contains several shelf heights, it's likely that you will *never* readjust the shelving. And fixed shelving eliminates the rows of holes required for adjustable shelving. Shelves hung at 18 in. to 30 in. above a work space can also double as a mount for task lighting.

Prefabricated shelving is now available in a variety of materials, but wood and engineered wood (plywood, medium-density fiberboard, and particleboard) are still the most popular. If your personal style dictates something less traditional, glass shelving helps achieve a classic modern design (more on that later), and mobile or fixed-wire shelf units are favorites in increasingly popular restaurant-style kitchens. Wire shelving makes a lot of sense for storing foods like root vegetables and fruit because it allows for better circulation than solid shelves, but you'll have to incorporate baskets or other containers for storing small items that could slip between wires. Plastic-coated wire shelving is widely available and can be assembled by a dedicated do-it-yourselfer, making it very cost-effective, although its humble aspect makes it more suitable for pantries and closed cabinetry than exposed areas.

Wood shelves Wood and engineered wood shelves are available in a range of styles and prices, making them a practical solution in the kitchen. But if they are asked to carry a heavy load without a proper support system, the

▲**Custom-made, wood-and-steel shelves** make a home for useful and decorative items. The unusual, pyramid-shaped shelves are a work of art in their own right. A tiny, metal pouch attached to the wall accents the bottom corner of the shelves, while providing storage space for kitchen scissors.

results can be disastrous. Wood shelves should be carefully selected according to your depth and width requirements in conjunction with the intended method of support; for instance, you don't want to store cast-iron pots on a long shelf with no intermediate supports. When sturdier shelving is required, brackets can be added at one or more points across the mid-span of the shelf. A cleat, which attaches to the wall and runs the length of the shelf, can be used to help prevent widthwise sag. Additionally, an edge band attached to the front of the shelf provides a considerable amount of stiffness by acting as a miniature support beam (see the drawing on p. 176).

Wood and engineered wood shelves can be finished with paint, stain, or a clear or tinted varnish or polyurethane—whatever personal preference calls for. On a practical note, however, city dwellers may prefer to use paint on fixed pantry shelves, eliminating any gap between shelf and wall, thus providing fewer hiding places for the wily cockroach. Just remember that when shelves are freshly painted—gloss

▼**The dramatically** cantilevered shelves in this Mexican-influenced house join the kitchen and dining area and create a bold display niche for folk art.

A Traditional Fixed Shelf

A cleat provides support along the entire length of the shelf, including the ends, if the shelf spans wall to wall.

An edge band isn't found on all pantry shelves, but it's invaluable for long spans. The band adds considerable strength and stiffness and gives a look of heft. But it can hamper taking tall items off the shelf.

Shelf brackets—available in many profiles—allow a shelf much longer overall span, and add to a traditional look.

▲ **A display niche with chunky glass shelves** and dramatic lighting fills the nook between kitchen and dining area.

or semigloss paint works best—you'll have to wait a while to load up the shelves. Wait at least as long as the paint-can label suggests, and then lay sheets of waxed paper (not plastic wrap) loosely (no tape) on the shelves before stocking them. After a while, slide the waxed paper out. This prevents the paint-stuck-to-the-soup-can problem, and works for all painted and stained shelves.

Glass shelves While wood may be the most popular material for shelves, glass can be an intriguing alternative, whether for stand-alone shelves or for shelves in cabinetry. They're particularly suitable for storing glassware and fine dishware that could be overwhelmed by dark and heavy wood shelves. Glass is also a boon in perpetually overcast climates or in rooms without a lot of windows, as it allows light to bounce around.

The edges of a glass shelf figure prominently in its overall look, so edge treatment and glass type should be carefully considered. Standard clear glass actually has a greenish tint, which is especially apparent at the edge; if you prefer a clearer glass, look for low-iron Starfire glass.

Glass shelves can be quite strong, but they have limits: A shelf with a light load and a short span can be a minimum of ⅜ in. thick, but longer spans (over 3 ft.) and heavier loads, such as stacks of plates, require a thickness of ½ in. or more. A glass fabricator or cabinetmaker can recommend the appropriate thickness. And while building codes don't generally require tempered glass in cabinet shelves, it's a good idea to check with your local building department.

Countertop Storage

A good rule for a hardworking kitchen is to keep countertops clear of as much clutter as possible. That said, the countertop can still provide valuable storage space. According to several kitchen-use studies, a countertop is at a good

▼ **When glass objects are** displayed on glass shelves, light gets a chance to bounce around. These shelves are supported by metal rods (which reflect light, too) but note the rubber O-rings, which lift the glass above the metal.

Remodeling History

Architects Rick and Liz O'Leary bought this 200-year-old cottage in a severely dilapidated condition, but over the last decade they've been nursing it back to life, room by room, as their budget allows. Their overriding design philosophy is to maintain a historic feel, but to mix it up with a few modern touches. Starting with the kitchen, they knocked out both exterior walls to install double-hung windows and a side door that leads to a new kitchen garden. Rick and Liz then plastered the upper part of the walls and installed wainscoting of wide-board, horizontal panels and ripped off a drywall ceiling to reveal existing timber beams. The last finish task was to replace the wide-board floor, which had been covered with sheet vinyl, and paint it with a handsome diamond pattern.

When the backdrop was complete, it was time to get down to the business of kitchen storage. The O'Learys put months of elbow

▲ **Two rolling, metal carts were fitted with butcher-block tops for extra prep space.**
Wire shelves hold cookbooks, spices, oils, hot pads, and other necessities for cooking.
The carts fit neatly on the sides of this restored restaurant range.

◀Two sets of beat-up drawers from a 1930s stationery store were thoroughly restored and fitted with new pulls. Matching cabinetry with inset doors was built and installed under the restored, porcelain cast-iron sink.

▲The restored drawers and new cabinets provide a punchy contrast to the white sink, marble countertop, and wall-mounted shelves. The newly built island is finished with more elaborate panels and painted a contrasting white. Simple wood towel bars hang from brackets at each end of the island.

grease into refinishing several kitchen pieces, including a cast-off restaurant range and a set of old drawers, which they painted dark blue and fitted with new bin pulls that are nickel-plated to match the restored 1920s faucet. They built wall-hung shelf units with adjustable shelves and base cabinets with inset doors, which support the two-bowl, reclaimed porcelain cast-iron sink. Countertops are made of Carrera marble salvaged from a local stone yard, which had mined it from an abandoned, half-built bakery. The finishing touch was two small, rolling metal carts

fitted with butcher-block tops that could be wheeled over to the range or out of the way.

This setup worked fine for a few years until one, and then two, little boys joined the household. A surge in at-home cooking required a dishwasher and more preparation space. To accommodate both in style, Rick wrapped two knocked-down base cabinets with ¾-in. plywood and then applied a face frame with panel molding. A dishwasher fits into one cabinet while drawers fit into the other.

◄**Don't let so-called leftover** space go to waste. Here, a niche behind a corner sink holds decorative objects, but it can do double duty as temporary storage for fruits and vegetables waiting to be washed, or for a recipe holder.

▲**A slot in the countertop** allows vegetable trimmings to be scraped directly into a container for composting.

working height if it comes up to just below your bent elbow (and about 4 in. lower for a pastry surface). On a countertop situated at that height, you'll use the first 18 in. of its depth comfortably, which leaves 6 in. of potential storage space at the back of the standard 2-ft. countertop. But use the back 6 in. sparingly, because it can be a handy staging area when cooking. Frequently used cooking utensils (in a sturdy jar) and small appliances are good candidates for countertop storage because they don't take up too much space, and having them nearby while cooking makes food preparation a less frantic affair. A narrow shelf—or even two—at the back of the countertop makes a useful addition, providing an out-of-the-way but accessible spot for spices, measuring cups, a kitchen timer, and other small kitchen tools that can quickly clog up a counter.

▲**This countertop exposes** its real-life job of making a home for appliances, fruits and vegetables, bakery leftovers, and a repotting in progress. Yet, there is still plenty of room to work.

◄**Maximize countertop** space by storing a pullout cutting board in a custom-made slot just under the countertop.

The Essential Pantry

Pantries are necessities once again in the American kitchen as we follow our ancestors' buying-in-bulk habits. Instead of visiting the general store on occasion for barrels of flour and sugar, we're shopping every few weeks at discount warehouse stores, hauling home super-sized bags of dog food and 27-count flats of bottled sports drink. Where to put these bulky nonperishables but in a pantry?

A pantry can be any size or configuration. If space is really tight but you still prefer to stockpile items, designate a longer-term pantry in a lesser-used space, such as the basement or even a garage (make sure items won't freeze or spoil from heat), and keep a small stash of items in the kitchen. A standard 2-ft.-deep closet can be converted into a pantry by installing rows of shelves that wrap around the walls. If no closet is available, carve out space between wall studs (avoiding electrical conduit and plumbing, of course) to fit a bookcase-like pantry, with or without doors.

The least efficient pantry arrangement is the standard fixed-shelf setup in a 2-ft.-deep base cabinet with doors or a 15-in.-deep wall cabinet—the food storage method that many of us grew up with (and that our parents cursed). If you must use a base cabinet, install pullout shelves. A similar option is pullout pantries, which are available prefabricated or which can be custom built. Pullouts use space quite efficiently because they neatly fit in spaces that are too small to accommodate a standard cabinet, and when the pantry is pulled out, it's easy to see all the items it contains. It's important to make sure, however, that the slides—the hardware that the pantry glides on—can handle the weight of the fully extended pantry shelves.

▼**Squeeze in storage space,** but not at the expense of comfort. This tiny kitchen is actually twice the size it was, but the designer refrained from boxing it in by making the end cabinets triangular. This opens up the kitchen to the table and actually provides the proper shallow shape for pantry storage.

Cabinet manufacturers also offer fold-out pantries, which include several vertical layers of narrow shelving. These can hold a lot of food, but they're relatively expensive, require a fair amount of widthwise space, can be slow to operate, and require a lot of forethought in the arrangement of items to ensure that none get lost or forgotten. A step-in pantry built on site can fit in the same amount of space for a much smaller price tag. Of course, the walk-in pantry is the queen of pantries, and if you can afford the space, you won't regret having one. Use an assortment of baskets, tins, or wood boxes inside a walk-in to store small items more efficiently, and a small table or countertop makes a useful addition as it can perform double duty as a secondary work space or makeshift bar.

Pantry shelves should be wide enough to hold one to four items front to back but narrow enough so that you can see what's on the shelves easily. Shelves around eye height should be no wider than 12 in. and can be much less, depending on the size of the pantry and what's being stored. Lower shelves can be deeper—even 20 in.—for bulkier items. Take a cue from the grocery-store stockers and stack items front-to-back first and then side-to-side.

Whatever style of pantry you have, make sure it's well lit. Pullout pantries are illuminated by general kitchen lighting, but a can of soup can be easily lost in the gloom of a multi-layer foldout pantry. A small light fixture that comes on when the door is opened can be installed in these units. A hanging or wall-mounted fixture works best in a step-in or walk-in pantry because it will evenly illuminate all (or most) of the shelves; a compact fluorescent bulb provides the best combination of economy and looks, and it gives off less heat.

▼ **This pantry is the center-**piece of a large opening that's framed by sleek cabinets. The walk-in pantry holds dishes on one side and food on the other. Shelves are ¾-in. plywood with edge-to-edge black-metal brackets.

Storing Kitchen Gear

It doesn't matter if you store a pot in a cabinet, on a shelf, or on a hook. What really counts is storing it close to its point of use and making it easy to retrieve, use, and put away. Ideally, this applies to everything stored in a kitchen. Pots and pans should be stored near the cooktop, baking sheets near the countertop where you make cookies, and dishware next to the sink and dishwasher. Cooking tools can be sorted in drawers located near the stove, or they can be stored out in the open in crockery or on hooks. It's good to keep in mind, however, that anything stored out in the open is going to gather dust and grease if it isn't used and washed daily. It's also good to keep in mind the laws of gravity; when loading shelves or cabinets, place heavier items below lighter ones.

▲ A lively kitchen for a serious cook has much of its storage out front—on pot racks, in big drawers, and on shelves tucked wherever possible.

◀ Built-in storage in this kitchen provides visual variety, pairing light wood wall cabinets with dark, plastic-laminate base cabinets, open shelves with doors, and wide shelves with a vertical stack of narrow shelves.

▼►**An urban house/art** studio in Oakland, California, has a kitchen designed for a couple of cooks, and a living/dining area designed for a group. Shelves under the cooktop hold bowls and other kitchen gear, while pots and pans are stored on a rack.

Pots and Pans

Store pots and pans according to their use first (are they used on the range top or in the oven?) and then by shape and size. Stockpots, pasta pots, and other big pots go together, saucepans together, sauté and frying pans together, and baking pans together. Among baking pans, stack round with round, square with square, rectangular with, well, you get the picture; pot lids can be stored in slotted racks or on hooks, just not on the pots themselves. More shelves with fewer items are a much less precarious (and annoying) option than one towering stack of pots and pans.

Pot racks Pot racks can be an appealing alternative to cabinet storage, particularly if you're a gear-head and enjoy viewing your collection. A pot rack belongs near the stove but not right over it, unless you like cleaning grease from pots you haven't even used. It's better to hang the rack over a nearby countertop or over an island, just as long as it's only a few steps from the cooktop. If the rack is hung over a work space, coordinate it with overhead lighting so that it doesn't cast annoying shadows. And another thing to consider—pot racks can't be hung on sky hooks, so before you get your heart set on a spot, make sure there are accommodating ceiling joists or wall studs. The height

Cooks' Kitchens

You can recognize the kitchen of an enthusiastic cook by the way cooking gear rules the roost: Tools are stored in jars on the counter or hung near the stove, pots are within easy reach, and cabinetry is designed to perform specific functions. These two kitchens are true cooks' kitchens with well-devised storage. In both kitchens, the cook's life is made easier by open shelves and slots for pots, plenty of rods for dish towels, and convenient storage for kitchen tools located where they are used or cleaned. In the white kitchen, space over the sink is fitted with teak slats that keep pans at the ready for cooking, while also serving as a dish rack. In the cherry kitchen, the backsplash is filled with shallow shelves that hold small appliances, spices, and bowls—a perfect setup for

▲**Rather than relegate the breakfast table** to a corner, this kitchen makes it the centerpiece. The low table is also the perfect height for rolling piecrust and kneading dough.

▲**Slots above the preparation** sink are fitted with teak slats that allow pans to drain into the sink. The pans remain in the slots until they are used again.

mise en place, the culinary term for making sure all ingredients and tools are ready before cooking. And in both kitchens, well-placed shelves make the most of storage space without interfering with the rooms' flow. In the white kitchen larger structures, like the breakfast table and pantry, are incorporated into the kitchen's active work space; they are both functional and attractive, which creates a hardworking, but still handsome, room.

▲**Abundant shelves situated above** and below the counter keep this kitchen uncluttered and operating smoothly. This smartly designed shelving unit stops short of the ceiling, which creates a display area for plants and baskets and doesn't block the windows behind it.

▲▲**A pantry that gets plenty of use needs** no door, like this one that adds a point of interest and easy access.

▲**This colorful pot rack,** which floats over a dainty-legged island table, makes a bright counterpoint to the colossal range and dark cabinets.

of the pot rack will depend on how far you can comfortably reach to take a pan off the rack safely, and to hook it back on.

Baking sheets and trays Storing trays and cookie sheets horizontally in stacks can make anyone give up and order out. A combination of the nesting instinct and gravity take hold of the stack, making it hard to grab just one pan and slide it out. Small slots that hold one or two trays are an improvement, but the best storage method is a series of vertical slots that hold a couple of trays or sheets apiece. A good place for this type of system is on top of the refrigerator, positioned flush with the front of the fridge, so it's easy to reach and doesn't get blocked by other items.

▲**Storage for flat objects,** such as trays and baking sheets, is easiest to access when it's vertical—in this case, over a refrigerator. The cabinet extends to the refrigerator's edge so that nothing can be stashed in front of it.

▲**In this kitchen, most appliances and utensils** are stashed in drawers and on shelves. But the pots and pans are perfectly situated on this rack, which is within easy reach of the stove but away from its grease and dust.

Another option is to outfit one of the leftover spaces between base cabinets (ideally next to the baking or food-prep area) with vertical slots, which makes great use of otherwise wasted space. Wherever the unit is located, consider the pros and cons of a door: For fast access and restaurant-style charm, leave the slots open, but if you don't use baking sheets frequently, specify a door to keep the space dust-bunny free.

▲**An all-drawer kitchen features light wood with retro metal** pulls. Shallow drawers handle knives and other cooking tools, while deep drawers carry heavy items—pots and pans—or bulky items, such as linens, or all those plastic odds-and-ends that seem to accumulate.

Small Tools

Avid cooks tend to prefer storing their cooking tools close at hand so they're easily retrievable. Tools on display are also a pleasure both for their beauty and for the sheer joy of ownership. (Who wouldn't want a rack of copper pots—and someone to clean them?) It costs much less to store tall, slender tools, such as wooden spoons and spatulas, in a heavy crock placed on the counter rather than in a custom-made drawer for the same number of tools. Plus, they're handier on the counter; it takes only one movement to grab a spoon from a jar versus three movements to retrieve one from a drawer—open drawer, rummage, grab tool. Tongs in particular are a nightmare to keep in a drawer, and they can even get tangled in a crock; if you use them often, you might consider storing them on their very own hook.

▲▲**A fanciful cutout on this island makes** stashing or retrieving a dish towel quick and easy.

An Abundance of Hidden Storage

This kitchen has a wealth of storage in a variety of guises. The continent-sized island handles a tremendous amount of storage with face-frame cabinets and inset doors and drawers, while perimeter cabinets against the wall have flush overlay doors and drawers. Throughout the kitchen, super-long handles double as dish-towel racks (but only on cabinet doors, as the towels would interfere with drawers). Three of the aluminum panels at the backsplash flip up to reveal an appliance garage fit for a four-star chef. The countertop has a full 2 ft. of clearance here, with the appliance garage recessed into the space behind the kitchen wall.

To brighten both cabinet contents and the kitchen itself, wall cabinets near the breakfast table have glass-door fronts and windows for backs, and all the other wall cabinets are fitted with halogen puck lights on top.

▲With appliance garage doors closed, the kitchen is a bright, serene space with volumes of storage and no clutter in sight.

▲Diner-style aluminum panels flip up, revealing a super-deluxe appliance garage. An outlet in the back keeps cords out of the way.

▲An extra-wide appliance garage under the microwave salvages counter space in this kitchen, which was remodeled in the style of Greene and Greene, hence the super-wide cabinet frames.

If you prefer a pristine, minimalist countertop (or for smaller tools that would get lost in a jar), designate a shallow drawer for tool storage in the vicinity of where they'll be used. The drawer should have enough dividers to keep like-sized tools aligned, but overcustomizing it with molded slots for every tool will backfire. Putting away utensils will turn into a shape-sorter toy—fun for a preschooler but a headache for a busy cook. It's also wise to have a couple of hooks near the oven for hot pads and a rod near the sink for dish towels. Extras can be stored in a drawer or bin nearby, perhaps with other essentials like storage bags, aluminum foil, waxed paper, and plastic wrap, which should be kept within easy reach of the food preparation area to make food storage and cleanup a breeze.

Small Appliances

Small appliance storage should follow the same guidelines as all other storage. It doesn't matter whether you choose to store small appliances in the open or in a cabinet as long as they're easily accessible. The coffee grinder can find a com-

▲This "one-car" appliance garage is just tall and wide enough for the bread machine, which is the largest of the small appliances and notoriously tricky to store.

▲A standard-sized appliance garage creates a coffee-making station with everything you need at hand—a certain blessing first thing in the morning.

fortable home in a wall cabinet or on a shelf above the coffee pot, depending on which space works best in the layout of your kitchen. One thing to keep in mind, however, is that frequently used appliances should be kept at eye level or below—it's unsafe (and inconvenient) to store them too high.

There are those of us who love to see certain appliances in a permanent place on the countertop, even if they take up useful space and collect crumbs and dust. If you are attached to the looks of a stand mixer, just find a quiet corner for it. And if you find it more convenient to keep most small appliances and other kitchen gear out in the open, consider 30-in.-deep countertops. (Cabinets that deep may not function well, aside from being extra expensive, so simply have the cabinets pulled out from the wall 6 in. and use that dead space for conduit or plumbing if needed. Any exposed cabinet sides will need an extra-deep panel to cover the gap.)

Some cooks prefer to stash small appliances in an appliance garage that is, so to speak, on grade with the countertop. While it, too, takes up counter space, a garage keeps appliances cleaner and more contained so that they don't spill out into your work space. Even small appliances that are used daily can be stored conveniently in an appliance garage—just don't park items in front of the garage or the stored items will be hard to back out. Whether you store appliances on the back of the countertop, in an appliance garage, or in a pantry, it's important to make sure you designate enough room for the tallest, a blender or bread-making machine, for instance.

Silver, Flatware, and Knives

Flatware or silverware stores nicely in drawers that are 4 in. to 5 in. deep. If you're purchasing custom-made cabinets and your cabinetmaker offers divided trays, opt for removable inserts, which allow for easier cleaning, and stackable trays, which provide a good spot for extra place settings. If you have oversized flatware or silverware, make sure the

◀**Shallow drawers work** best for cutlery and flatware because there's less opportunity for tangling. On the left, there's a concealed lower level perfect for seasonal utensils like ice-tea spoons and lobster crackers.

▲**A Craftsman-style drawer** and its flatware insert were designed with characteristic dovetail corners—a handsome and sturdy detail.

cabinetmaker is aware of the size slots or partitions required. Divider trays are widely available in home stores, too, but remember to test your own settings to make sure they fit before you buy.

Silverware Cabinetmakers may offer silvercloth-lined drawers for storing silver, either with slots for each piece or compartments for groups of pieces. Additional, loose storage cloths will come in handy as well. Silvercloth, which traps the airborne chemicals that tarnish silver, is also available by the yard if you want to line an existing drawer. (Don't use glue containing sulfur, which tarnishes silver.) In addition to silvercloth, drying silver immediately after washing it will go a long way to prevent tarnish.

Knives Safety is a prime concern with knife storage, and that includes storing them in a manner that doesn't dull the blade—a dull knife resists slicing and can easily slip. And even though Julia Child uses a magnetic strip, this isn't an ideal choice for storing knives because it exposes knives to moisture and hasty, careless handling, which can damage the blade. Slots in the back of a countertop and slotted butcher-blocks are much safer methods, although some chefs claim that poking a knife into a slot can dull the blade, and a blade that chews its way through the block can scratch the countertop. It's also nearly impossible to thoroughly clean a butcher block. The safest method of knife storage is a lockable drawer fitted up with a shallow, slotted wood block. A knife is slipped into the slot smoothly along the whole blade rather than point first.

Storing Dishes and Glassware

Dishes and glassware obviously have more eye appeal than soup cans (for most of us, anyway), so these are the items to show off in the kitchen. Cabinets with glazed doors—frosted for a subtle look and clear for dishes that always look great and stack neatly—are a great option, or even cabinets with no doors at all. Particularly attractive collections can be stored on open shelving separate from the cabinetry to create a showcase effect. Even everyday dishes can benefit from open shelves, especially if they're within reach of the dishwasher, which will make unloading the beast a much less painful task. Freestanding hutches and china cabinets provide attractive and safe storage for fine china and fancy serving pieces.

Incorporating adjustable ceiling spot lighting or cabinet lighting will highlight your collection and make it easier to retrieve what you need. Cabinet lights can be

▼**A shallow drawer below** the cooktop handles tools, while a deep drawer holds pots and pans. A knife slot is built directly into the countertop for handy and safe storage—the blades run down behind the open shelving below.

◄ **Dish storage to die for: two cabinets with** doors and shelves and two with glazed doors hold an abundance of dishes and glasses. The cabinets are positioned in a corner of the kitchen, next to the serving countertop and on the way to dining.

▲ **Plate racks are available off-the-shelf** in several styles, or they can be custom-made in any size and style you'd like. This rack has graceful curves and a row of pegs for cups.

switched on remotely or designed to turn on when you open the cabinet. Even though they're not the most glamorous members of the kitchen, base cabinets can benefit from lighting as well. Anyone who's ever muttered a silent oath while blindly searching through a deep base cabinet for the turkey platter knows that installing a door-operated light is a true blessing.

Dishes Even if space is limited, try to avoid stacking different types of dishes together, luncheon plates on top of dinner plates, for instance. Various types of plates and bowls are needed throughout a family's day, and there's a higher risk of breakage when you have to pull something out from under a stack; storing the same size dishes together in a single stack is the safest and most functional option. The same goes for storing everyday dishes and their more formal cousins. Cramming fine dishes together with the workhorse variety is a recipe for disaster. Fine dishes and serving pieces

◀**A bright collection of dishes** deserves to be seen, and these cabinets sport glass doors and halogen lights, perfect for displaying. Plates find a haven in a built-in rack.

▲**An unusual, round window invites light into** this kitchen, highlighting the adjacent shelves. Because they're on open shelving, the glasses are stored upside down to deter dust. The shelves have been placed at different heights to accommodate everything from petite wine glasses to hefty beer steins.

should get their own home far away from the hurried hands of a busy family, and you can further protect them from chips and scratches by stacking them between layers of felt, soft foam, a special plate pad, or even a paper towel.

Glasses Glasses do well in both open and closed storage units, but they require different care, depending on where you put them. Glasses stored in open cabinets or on open shelves will collect dust unless they're stored upside down. Regardless of storage location, stacking glasses should be avoided if at all possible, but if you must, these guidelines will keep accidents to a minimum. For straight-sided glassware, place one glass upside down, and stack the second right side up on top of it. In the case of tapered glasses, stack no more than three inside each other, and avoid stacking a warm-from-the-dishwasher glass inside a cold glass—it may be difficult to extract later because the warm glass swells. It's fine to hang everyday teacups from hooks and even to stack them, but finer china will fare better if set singly on a protected shelf.

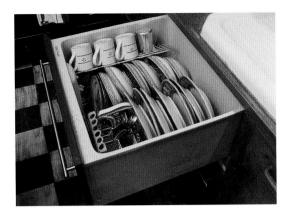

▲ **This dishwasher drawer requires no bending** over to load. At half the size of a standard dishwasher, it makes sense for small families who would either waste water and energy on a half-full standard dishwasher, or who would have to wait several days until the washer was full before running a load.

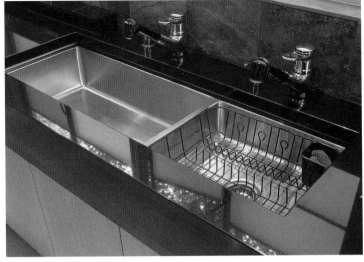

▲ **This sink is a cook's dream, with plenty of room to wash** vegetables and stash a good-sized wire drainer—no throwing high-quality cooking gear in the dishwasher in this kitchen.

Drying space for hand-washed dishes It's rare to see a plastic-coated wire dish drainer with a plastic drainboard on a fancy kitchen tour or in a home-design publication (though you'll find a few bold examples in this chapter). But look under the sink and you'll probably find one—it's a rare kitchen, no matter how fancy, that doesn't require a place to drain dishes and pots. Paper towels strewn across the countertop aren't an ideal alternative from an aesthetic or practical point of view, especially considering the variety of attractive dish-drying racks and drainboards on the market. Some racks are simply decorative and the slots aren't actually wide enough for dishes, odd as that may seem, so take a few dishes to the store for a trial run. It's ideal to sit the drying unit in one side of a two-bowl sink, but if that's not an option, situate the rack and drainboard on the side of the sink, and allocate a hidden space for it when not in use. Or get one that's as aesthetically pleasing as it is necessary and embrace the notion of beauty born of functionality.

▲ **Unpretentious but attractive, this dish-drying** rack simply rests on a stainless-steel counter covered by a pretty dish towel; Arts and Crafts-style glass cabinets above hold dry dishes.

A butler's pantry If you entertain frequently and have enough space, consider storing glassware and dishes in a butler's pantry, a common feature of large and modest 19th- and early-20th-century homes. This space, positioned between kitchen and dining room, contained cabinetry and countertops. Food was plated here, and dishes, glasses, and serving pieces were washed and stored here, often in glass-front cabinets. Table linens and large serving pieces were stored in base cabinets fitted with drawers or shelves. Fragile, expensive china, crystal, and silver were never allowed in the hot, dusty, greasy environment of the strictly utilitarian kitchens of yore but were housed solely in the butler's pantry under close supervision. Despite the modern trend of large eat-in kitchens, the butler's pantry can still be quite useful, offering a wealth of backup storage and work space, as well as a shield for dirty dishes during a dinner party until the butler (that's you, dear) arrives to wash up.

▲ ▶ **It doesn't take much floor space to build** a modern-day butler's pantry; this one benefits from a large, round window that lights up the collection of glassware. A hinged, narrow shelf between the pantry and the dining area makes a perfect sidebar.

Storing Foods

Just take a good look inside your cabinets and pantry. How many brands of cereal do you see? Then count the shapes of pasta, types of cat food, bottles of barbecue sauce and sesame oil. And so forth. While our forefathers merely stored huge quantities of a few items (barrels of apples, cellars-full of turnips), we have huge quantities of a mind-boggling variety of items. How we store them can contribute greatly to the sanity of a household. It's ideal to store like items together, but if you have a year's supply of soft drinks, store a few cans in the kitchen and the balance in bulk storage wherever you can make room. Store bulk items in a built-in pantry next to the kitchen, in a designated pantry section of a cool, dry basement, or even in a temperate garage. A skilled grocery-store bagger separates cold foods from dry goods, which is a good rule of thumb if you're packing your own, because it's easier to unload and put away once you get home.

Storing Cold Food

The refrigerator is a major player in kitchen storage, both in terms of what it stores and how it looks, but it doesn't have to throw its weight around anymore.

▲ **A pullout pantry next to** the refrigerator and cooktop provides instant gratification to a cook.

◀**This refrigerator, finished** in rich, Craftsman-style mahogany panels, has the typical shelf and door storage inside. Below are two freezer drawers with matching mahogany panels. Dividing the freezer in this manner makes the unit less bulky and more accessible.

▲**Potatoes and onions will** spoil quickly if stored together, so simply store them in separate drawers or containers, preferably in a cool spot.

Over the past decade, refrigerators have slimmed down, split off from their freezer siblings, and donned the trappings of upscale cabinetry, although there will always be a small but fanatical following of advocates for the rough-and-tough, restaurant-style behemoths. Today's refrigerators look different on the inside, too, with more compartments and individual climate controls for various foods and shelves that can be adjusted—even when loaded with food—or flipped up and out of the way to handle unusual space needs, such as chilling a few bottles of champagne. Your individual needs and habits will dictate which model will be the most efficient in your kitchen.

The basic refrigerator/freezer types haven't changed—there are the top-mount freezers, the bottom-mount freezers, and the side-by-side units. The side-by-side is the least energy and space efficient, and you may find the narrow refrigerator shelves frustratingly limited, but they make it easy to install water and ice dispensers, and the narrow doors interfere less with kitchen traffic. The latest versions of side-by-side refrigerator/freezers may have solved the "no-room-for-a-platter" problem by making the refrigerator

▲**These refrigerator drawers** were installed under the microwave so that produce would be close to the food-preparation countertop.

▲**A freezer and refrigerator** don't have to be joined at the hip. In this setup, they are separated by a corner cupboard. Additional refrigerator drawers are located beneath the units and are tempered to handle the specific needs of produce and dairy products.

wider at the top (doors are offset to accommodate the different widths).

Perhaps because it is generally more expensive than the top-mount freezer model, the bottom-mount freezer unit is the least common of the three, even though it's the most energy efficient and the easiest to access since you're in the refrigerator much more often than the freezer. And as we've discovered with cabinets, drawers can be more practical than doors and shelves, because it's easier to pull out the drawer and bend over than to squat and rummage blindly for the ice cream. Some models offer two freezer drawers, which helps organize food storage even more.

Refrigerator/freezer units can be freestanding or built in. Freestanding models are usually deeper (because the compressor is on the back) and less expensive than built-ins. Many companies are making shallower, freestanding models to suit the preference for slim-refrigerator styles with a more modest price tag. It's possible to outfit a freestanding refrigerator with cabinetry for a built-in look, but it's important to allow breathing room around all three sides to vent the compressor. It's also possible to embellish a freestanding fridge itself with panels that match the cabinets, or you can choose a contrasting material, such as stainless steel. (Remember that standard refrigerator stainless steel won't hold magnets, so request high-ferrous steel for storing snapshots and kid art on the fridge. An easier, neater route is to designate a space in the kitchen for a corkboard or magnetic board.) Built-in refrigerator/freezers are shallower than their chunkier, freestanding relatives, so they fit seamlessly into the standard, 2-ft.-deep run of cabinetry. They are taller, too, because the compressor is usually located on top, which requires a ventilation panel.

▼In this tiny (91 sq. ft.) kitchen, the refrigerator is encased in a pantry unit for ultra-efficient use of space. The refrigerator is a small and energy-saving unit made by Vestfrost (since renamed Conserv), which uses very little electricity and has two compressors, one for the refrigerator and one for the freezer, so both spaces don't have to be recooled when one door is open.

◄**A gently curving alcove** contains a range, lots of unencumbered work space, and convenient spice storage. Taking a cue from restaurant kitchens, it even has a warming shelf for plates.

Like built-in refrigerator/freezer units, the latest refrigerator and freezer components are built-ins and can be finished to match or contrast with the kitchen cabinetry. Refrigerator drawers are relatively pricey, but they make a lot of sense. You can situate the drawers where they are most needed; produce can be placed near the prep sink and cutting board, while dairy products can be stored near the breakfast nook so that getting the milk doesn't require a trek through the kitchen. Separating food groups also allows the foods to be stored at their optimum temperature and humidity. You'll still need a (smaller, perhaps) standard refrigerator unit with a door and shelves for storing condiments, leftovers, and trays of party food, however. But this could even be one of the compact under-counter refrigerators, which are much more energy efficient and capacious than the models we had in college.

Storing Spices

It's not uncommon to see a spice rack hanging next to the stove, but that's not an ideal setup. Heat and light quickly degrade herbs and spices, so it's best to store them in a cool,

▲**This cooking alcove,** devised of steel and green tile, keeps everything the cook needs close by. The spice rack's vicinity to the stove is fine for small amounts of frequently used spices, but bulk storage should happen elsewhere—preferably in a cool, dry place.

► **Spices stored over the oven?** Fine, as long as it's a microwave. With spices and knives within reach, this end-grain, butcher block workstation makes food preparation a smooth and easygoing affair.

▲ **This cabinet spice rack** is a work of art. The Finland birch frame is finished with prerusted steel and etched glass. The handle is—what else—a fish.

dark place if possible. Many cooks keep favorite spices next to the cooktop and store backup spices in cooler spots, sometimes in the refrigerator. Spice storage depends on your sense of style, the way you cook, and your spice-buying habits. You may prefer identical spice jars that fit into a drawer insert or on a rack attached to the inside of a cabinet door (make sure it clears the shelves), or conversely, decanted into opaque containers and stored in the open. If a spice collection includes various-sized jars, boxes, and bags, it will be neater to store them in a drawer (label the lids for easier identification) or on a pantry shelf. And if you have a large spice collection, you will not regret keeping containers in rough alphabetical order. Slender pullout shelves in a base cabinet—remember, within reach of the work space but not near a source of heat—are tailor-made for spices.

◄It's fine to store everyday wine in the kitchen as long as it doesn't sit for too long. In this kitchen, a wine rack was built into a base cabinet.

▲▲A simple-but-elegant wine rack like this one can be placed in the kitchen, dining room, or butler's pantry.

Storing Wine

The way most of us store wine would curl the lip of any oenophile. The kitchen is no place for long-term wine storage, unless you've invested in a wine cooler. These miniature wine cellars, which fit under the standard, 3-ft.-high countertop, chill wine to temperatures between 48°F and 60°F. Much larger wine credenzas with 200-bottle capacities can be fitted up like fancy cabinetry, making them an elegant addition to a bar area or large dining room.

A pantry may not be as glamorous as a wine cellar, but if it's well ventilated, dark, and reasonably cool, it beats storing wine in the kitchen proper. A cool, dry basement is perfect for wine storage, whether it's in inexpensive wine racks or cardboard boxes turned on their sides. If you like to collect good wine, investing in a wine cooler or setting up a small basement room with an air conditioner can be money well spent. Researching and collecting young wines and saving them until their prime brings joy to many peo-

▲A refrigerator drawer that's specifically calibrated for wine can provide short-term storage for a dinner party, or it can be used as a miniature wine cellar.

▶A mahogany wine cellar provides chilled storage for a thousand bottles of wine, plus a few wine tasters. A rack overhead keeps glasses dust-free and within reach. The door in the center background is a built-in humidor for cigar storage.

▲A steel frame with folded metal plates and steel cables creates a sculptural, short-term storage space for a few wine bottles in this Oakland, California, kitchen.

ple, especially if they can relish the fact that they paid half or even a tenth of a mature—or suddenly trendy—wine's shelf price. But hardly anyone will object to storing non-pedigreed wine in slots in kitchen cabinets, as long as such units aren't near any obvious hot spots and the wine is consumed fairly soon.

Trash and Recyclables

These days, there are a multitude of cabinet accessories for holding trash and recyclables of all sorts. The easiest type to use are pullout receptacles, which—thankfully—don't often fit under the sink, making cleanup a much more harmonious experience for two or more people. Pullout receptacles bring the trash out at the level of the countertop, so it's easy to dump in scraps without bending over. Some pullout accessories include a shelf below the trash container; this is

◀▼**Pullout trash drawers come in several** configurations, colors, and sizes. Multiple compartments allow for quick sorting.

a great spot for storing trash bags. Your community's requirements for sorting recyclables will determine what kind of containers you need. A really thirsty family may require a bin solely for recyclable containers, plus one for returns, but it's hard to justify space for these big containers in the kitchen. A mudroom or outdoor closet (one that nocturnal critters can't access) is a suitable home for large bins.

Cleaning Supplies

The unfortunate by-product of food is grease, grime, and trash. The kitchen is a major mess factory, so cleaning supplies should be kept in or very near the kitchen. You're much more likely to keep things clean if supplies are at hand. Under-the-sink storage is a common option, but powdered cleansers and dishwashing detergent won't fare well in dampness. Broom closets are available as accessories for

▲**This work surface has an under-counter** container to hold vegetable trimmings, which are dumped on the compost heap daily.

◄**Make every effort to store** trash somewhere other than under the sink; in this kitchen, it's stored in a pullout base-cabinet compartment for easy access.

Don't Forget a Fire Extinguisher

A fire extinguisher is a small item to store, but it can have a huge impact in a kitchen fire. It should be stored in an accessible location away from the stove, so it's easy (and safe) to grab during a fire. Ideally, an extinguisher should be mounted near an exit where it can be seen but is out of reach of children. A UL-listed, ABC, or all-purpose, extinguisher is a good choice for a kitchen. Do not depend on a fire extinguisher for anything but a small, contained fire, as it doesn't have the capacity for more than a few seconds of spray. The extinguisher should be charged after each use.

◄**The corner doesn't have** to be a tricky design problem. In this kitchen it's fitted with a divided, rotating trash container.

stock and custom cabinetry, but you can also build your own by designating space in the pantry for a broom, mop, vacuum, and bucket, with shelves (separate from food storage) for cleaning supplies. Wherever cleaning supplies are stored, make sure they're locked away from small children. If a central vacuum is on your wish list, remember to include the kitchen; a vacuum port can be mounted on a wall or cabinet end.

Beyond Basic Kitchen Gear

▲ **Despite its diminutive size, this cook's desk** still has room for a number of cookbooks. A thin glass cabinet squeezes in between desk and refrigerator.

The kitchen is frequently described as the heart of a home. And so it is, with many activities taking place besides food preparation. Today's kitchens often incorporate places to sit, talk, work, play, and even to sleep (a built-in bench can make a great spot for a nap). Our new kitchen habits require another layer of storage that goes beyond kitchen gear and makes space for books, stationery, art supplies, even toddler toys. While it can be tricky to find this much space, doing so boosts the kitchen's usefulness and makes it an even happier place to be. Part of the secret to making room for everything is finding storage space for kitchen gear in other rooms as well. For those who still have a separate dining room, this is the first place to look—think of it as an extension of the kitchen. And because no kitchen or dining space is whole without a bit of embellishment, there should be space dedicated to art and your favorite collections.

◄ **This hallway, a new** addition to a dark, colonial-style house, was a good investment, adding much needed light as well as additional storage for kitchen gear, linens, and kids' toys. It also reroutes traffic, keeping the kitchen clear of extraneous bodies. Yes, those are mailboxes over the cooktop.

▶ **This tiny desk is an** extension of the breakfast nook, but it offers enough room for a phone and a few cookbooks—all that's really needed from a kitchen desk.

▲ **This desk pays homage to its surroundings** by incorporating kitchen gear into its setup, with bread pans used for storing mail.

Room for a Desk

Even though it eats up a lot of space, a desk in a kitchen is easy to justify when you really think about it. A desk allows you to multitask, keeping an eye on dinner while paying bills or finishing up business. School-age kids can use the space for homework under a watchful eye, and smaller children can hunker down over an art project. If you like to cook, chances are you collect cookbooks, which can be stored near the desk for reading and comparing recipes. The desk should include all the usual nooks, like drawers for hanging files, a big drawer for phone books, and shallow drawers for pencils. A desk is an obvious place for the kitchen message center, so space for a phone and messages,

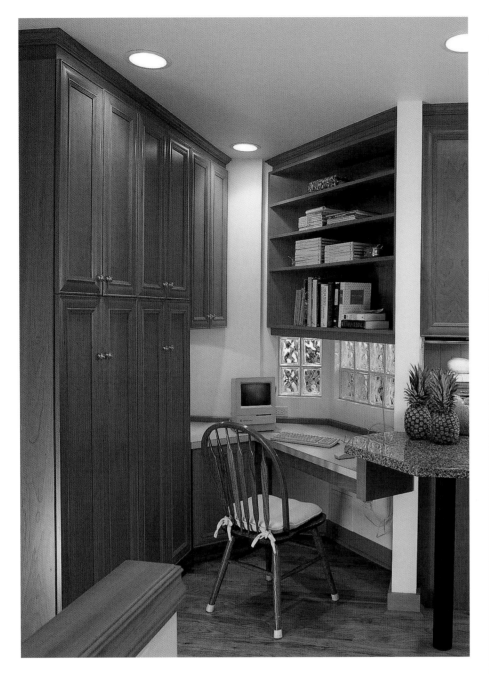

◄**Kitchen cabinets are angled to separate** the work area from the cook's desk, creating a cozy kitchen and a cozier place to read, write, or ponder life's mysteries.

whether on a tackboard, chalkboard, or both, should be included. If the kitchen desk includes a computer, leave part of the desk clean for other projects. Tuck computer accessories, such as a printer, on a shelf below the desk. A roll-down or tilt-in door can cover the desk work space during heavy-duty cooking sprees, or when company's coming.

▲**In this kitchen, the desk** is part of a built-in cabinetry unit, which makes it flow with the rest of the kitchen. The drawers are fitted for hanging files, and a corkboard helps keep track of important papers.

▼ ▶ **Books and pottery are displayed on** shelves that blend in with the wood paneling and look down on a breakfast banquette in this Arts and Crafts house. Across from the banquette is a window seat and a short wall of cabinetry that includes closed cabinets and open shelves.

Dining Spaces

Dining spaces can range dramatically in their character and use, but all dining spaces benefit from some storage capability. A breakfast nook or dining room with nothing but a table will suffer from disuse or disarray. Provide a built-in or freestanding sideboard for serving food, displaying large serving pieces, and storing table linens. Additional cabinets and hutches can accommodate runoff from the kitchen and will provide a secure location for china. If you don't need the extra storage, a dining-room cabinet may be the perfect spot for a sound system or to display art. And if you've been searching in vain for a place to put the bookshelf, the dining room may be just the place. A breakfast nook will benefit from a small bookshelf, too, and space to stack a few newspapers for peaceful, Sunday reading.

◀ **In this home, a family room** and dining area share space, but each is defined by a different floor level and set off by a hutch, which functions as both screen and storage area. Serving pieces, linens, and candles are stored in the hutch, and its top surface serves as a sideboard.

▼ **Rather than take up room** in the kitchen, finer china and glassware are stored in built-in cabinetry in the dining room, along with linens (in the wide, shallow drawers) and serving pieces. Recessing the cabinet makes it less obtrusive.

Plate Rails

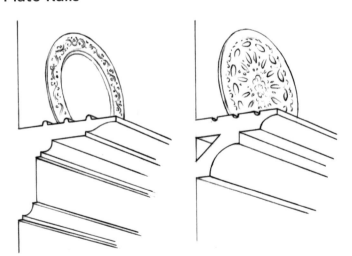

Plate rails are built up of stock molding parts; many configurations and styles are possible. Add brackets or dentils for more detail. Provide grooves or continuous beads on top of the rail to hold various-sized plates.

▲Dining-room shelves are plastered seamlessly into the wall, highlighting a collection of plates rather than the shelving itself.

Storing Art Collections

Kitchens and dining spaces frequently display collections of food-related objects that have a practical purpose, but there's nothing wrong with displaying art for art's sake, as well. Consider the relatively greasy and dusty atmosphere, however, and choose items wisely.

Collections will be shown to their best advantage if you create a purposeful space specifically for them, rather than just plunking them down on the windowsill. Plates and similarly shaped objects can be displayed on a high plate rail, a narrow shelf set on crown or bed molding; a groove or stop on the rail allows plates to lean against the wall without sliding off. Door frames can be given a flat top that extends the door profile and makes space for small collections, but be aware that closing doors can jar objects loose from their perch. Regardless of what you choose to display or how you display it, including art in your kitchen design will help it live up to its potential of being the heart of your home.

Living Spaces

E ven more so than the kitchen, today's living space must be a jack-of-all-trades. Whether we call it a family room, great room, or simply a living room (does anyone say parlor anymore?), living space is where people go to relax—alone, with family, or with guests. The room must accommodate a variety of activities, from reading the newspaper to watching the World Series, from having a quiet conversation to throwing an elegant party. This contrast of purpose presents a storage challenge. How do you store all the gear related to both entertaining and relaxing without overpowering a space that depends on its looks? Larger houses may be able to afford the space for spin-off living areas that host more specific functions, such as a sitting room or media room, but most living spaces must handle a range of solo and group activities all on their own.

Storage pieces, whether freestanding or built-in, can help organize living space so that it's better able to serve these multiple functions. Along with providing much needed storage space, freestanding and built-in furniture can be used to divide a living space into smaller components that

▶**This stepped *tansu*, a** traditional Japanese storage unit, accommodates the everyday stuff that would otherwise clutter this living room. Its steps also offer graduated storage display space.

◀**This room has a lived-in, welcoming feel, yet the less appealing paraphernalia of daily life is kept at bay in** smart—and attractive—storage. The fireplace acts as an anchor for two built-in storage units; the base cabinet of the right unit conceals clutter, while the base cabinet on the left holds the television. Bookshelves above provide a storage/display area for artful items, as does the fireplace mantel. The end table between couch and love seat offers temporary storage for drinks and a permanent home for a plant.

◀These Craftsman-style cabinets, in a nontraditional maple, brighten this bungalow's sitting-room addition. Half-height walls are topped with stout columns and fitted with display cases that are protected by decorative glazed doors. These walls separate the sitting and dining rooms without screening views and light.

▲A double row of books and building artifacts runs around the room on a high rail, which balances the high ceilings, making the room more intimate. Baskets and funky tables provide additional storage for books and other items.

can become more specialized. For instance, a large bookshelf, placed perpendicular to a wall, could partition off a computer desk from the living room where sofas and TV reside.

Freestanding furniture, such as armoires, chests, and tables, can subdivide a living space in less time and for less money than built-in pieces. Many of the living spaces featured in this chapter use furniture to carve up space while built-in cabinetry is limited to the room's perimeter. Built-in units, however, can be customized to your exact specifications, and personalized storage solutions pave the way for a truly organized home because they take into account your family's particular needs and habits.

Regardless of how you set up living space, it's essential to provide concealed storage to prevent clutter—the alternative is a coffee table that's buried under remote controls and a week's supply of newspapers. Concealed storage is also the likely harbor for a television and sound system plus all the accessories they require. Whether you decide

▲Handsome, arch-topped cabinetry in this well-used family room is home to all kinds of storage, including games, magazines, a sound system, mini-kitchen with refrigerator, trash receptacle, and dishware storage.

to use freestanding, built-in, or modular units in your living space, make sure the pieces have plenty of drawers or shelves with doors.

Along with closed storage for the things you don't want to see, living rooms should have ample display space for the things you do, like photographs, artwork, and collections.

Freestanding Storage

Built-in storage can take up a substantial amount of space, as well as take a whopping bite from your budget. And rightly so—it's an investment that will last. Free-standing furniture, on the other hand, offers instant gratification. It can be a less expensive, less permanent option that can be just as useful and dramatic as built-in furniture. As styles and needs change, freestanding furniture can be replaced and moved around, offering more flexibility and possibility. Armoires, hutches, bookcases, tables, trunks, and modular storage systems can be pushed from corner to corner, room to room, reshaping space as need dictates—and it can be carted right out of the house when you move.

▼Loft living: The raised bed/couch provides great storage for magazines—underneath. Tall sculptural frames play many roles, acting as headboard, screening part of the kitchen, and stretching to make bookcases and a sideboard near the dining table.

◀A living room in a Martha's Vineyard house doubles as a guest bedroom, with bolstered daybeds that also serve as couches. The storage chest can be a chessboard by day and bedside table by night, while the drawers hold chess pieces and additional board games.

Refreshment Center

If your living space isn't immediately adjacent to the kitchen, guests and family alike will appreciate a side table or cabinet dedicated to refreshment. An under-counter refrigerator (which can be paneled or tucked into a cabinet for aesthetics) holds soft drinks, mixers, and party drinks, while shelves provide storage for dishes and glassware. Drawers hold cocktail napkins or coasters, and the flat surface on top of the unit offers a place to set down a drink at a crowded party or a place for hors d'oeuvres. For quieter family affairs, the unit provides easy access to refills without pausing the movie or missing the winning touchdown.

While there's no exact combination of freestanding pieces that will guarantee smart storage, it's useful to have a range of storage options. Whatever pieces you choose, you'll have the most flexibility if you give yourself different types of storage—open and closed, shelves and drawers. An end table with a drawer provides a flat surface for drinks and a place for coasters, while a small chest with shelves and doors serves as a miniature wet bar. An armoire houses videos, DVDs, and CDs, while an antique seaman's trunk offers visual interest, as well as a home for extra blankets. Open shelves mounted at eye level safely display photographs and art.

Cabinets and Beyond

Freestanding cabinets, hutches, armoires, and chests provide a wealth of storage options. Whether antique or in keeping with the latest trends, this category of furniture can be found in nearly every style, size, and price range. Consider

Modular Storage Components

A popular and affordable way to customize living-room storage is with modular storage systems, now widely available from houseware companies. Modular storage systems have been around for a while, usually with modern styling.

Today's modular storage systems can be found in a number of styles and materials, including wire, metal, and panel products (plywood, medium-density fiberboard, and particleboard). These systems can be attached to a wall, but they're generally freestanding.

Modular units are touted for their variety and flexibility: You can plug together shelves, cubbies, and drawers at will and change them as needs change. They're a great storage option for growing families, where toddlers' toys will make way for older kids' toys, such as board games, video games, and music.

While many of us will never change our storage units once they're in place, it's comforting to know that we can easily swap a drawer for a shelf or three shelves for two. This versatility of design and the relative ease of installation make modular storage an ever-popular solution to our ever-growing collection of stuff.

how much of each storage type you need, and select pieces that speak to your sense of style and living habits. If you have small children, you'll probably need to focus on closed storage units; if the living space is also a play space, make sure that any tall, freestanding furniture is sturdy enough to withstand an onslaught of tumbling kids. If, however, your house is child-free, a unit with glass doors might be just the thing to show off a collection while protecting it from the elements. It's also important to choose pieces that complement the overall feel of a room. A towering, dark-wood armoire may be overpowering in an informal living space.

Older pieces of furniture, such as an inherited, heart-pine armoire or a black-walnut *tansu* discovered at an antique shop, can be retrofitted with stronger shelves and modern hardware to make them more sturdy and functional. But don't make such drastic changes to an antique cabinet that has real value to a collector or to your family. A better option may be to purchase fully modernized furniture rendered in a period style.

◀ **A handsome, antique** corner cupboard finds a new home in this charming, buttery living room. It provides the perfect hiding place for modern conveniences, such as a television or sound system.

Floor Outlets

For furniture placed against walls, it's easy to find outlets for electronic equipment and lighting. But a more comfortable, versatile living space is likely to have furniture placed away from the wall to make separate conversation and activity areas, so consider floor outlets (it's dangerous to cover electrical cords with carpets). You can custom-cut to handle the outlet and its brass plate, or simply position area rugs to avoid the floor outlet.

Tables

Tables are essential storage elements in a living room, primarily for short-term storage of games, reading material, and refreshments. To create a comfortable space for both entertaining and solitude, provide plenty of open table space for cups and saucers, glasses, and plates. Store coasters in plain sight or in an easy-to-reach drawer in a coffee, side, or end table. You'll find that drawers and shelves are real assets in living space tables—even a low coffee table can sport a bottom shelf for magazines or games in progress. Trunks and chests can double as coffee or side tables while providing the added bonus of abundant concealed storage space. Any table that's primarily used for display items should be placed out of traffic's way—at the corner of two perpendicular couches or in a corner of the room—to prevent jostling and to make it a little harder to plunk down a wet glass.

Built-In Storage

Built-in storage can rescue an architecturally drab or limiting living space in many ways. Built-ins can define space on a grander scale than freestanding furniture; they can be customized to suit your exact needs; and they can make a big splash in the looks department. Built-in furniture and cabinetry is generally more expensive than freestanding furniture, but it also increases the market value of a home. On the other hand, you can't take it with you if you move, and you can't change it if you get bored easily, so it's important to match the money you'll spend with an equal amount of forethought.

Built-in cabinets can be customized to fill small niches for individualized storage, or they can be built on a larger scale to create pseudo-walls that subdivide a room. When you design a bank of built-in cabinets, consider height and depth, complexity of pattern, and a balance of concealed and open storage. A unit that continues to the ceiling will

◀▲ **Living-room storage** flanks the entry hall, which is guarded by the family's "watch" dog. A formal, but simple arch ties together the nicely proportioned composition of open shelves and closed base cabinets. On the opposite side of the room are wide cabinets, set flush in a thick wall. The doors on these cabinets have a more complex design than the arched cabinetry but still complement its general design.

◀ **An impressive wall of** built-in storage runs from floor to 9-ft. ceiling, even stretching over a doorway. Closed cabinets are punctuated by arch-top, open shelves in this peaceful, English-style great room. Crown molding on the front of the unit runs the length of the wall and conceals fluorescent light fixtures attached to its top, which suffuse the ceiling with a warm glow.

▲ **Clerestory windows bounce light off the** ceiling above a deep row of display shelves in this contemporary living room. Other storage—the messy, utilitarian kind—is in sleek, closed cupboards below.

look like part of the wall itself, while stopping it short of the ceiling provides a space for display or lighting. In many cases, base cabinetry alone supplies ample storage, allowing room for a visual treat above—be it a window, piece of art, or elaborate mirror.

◄ **The site-built, millwork** shelves in this cottage living room are adjustable to accommodate a growing collection of design books. Cases between bookshelves cover electric baseboard units and provide extra space to stack books and display items, such as a vase of daisies.

▼ **Stretching across the long** wall of a modern great room, this bank of cabinetry is lightened by intervals of open space that create niches for *ikebana* (Japanese-style floral arrangements) and a piano.

The upper half of a wall-sized bank of built-in cabinets demands visual attention in a room, and if it's not in balance with the rest of the space, it may look disproportionate and overwhelming. A good way to lighten the effect of a large built-in is to use open shelving or cabinets with glass doors on top, which will also show off your more artful items to best effect. Objects displayed on visible shelves will further benefit from lighting, either within the cabinet or, if it's open shelving, from nearby spot lighting installed on the wall or ceiling.

The lower half of a large-scale built-in traditionally comprises base cabinets fitted with solid doors or drawers, and for good reason. Doors and drawers can be locked or child-proofed if necessary, and they can do the dirty work of masking potential disarray and items that just aren't that good-looking. The contrast between solid lower cabinets

and open upper cabinets or shelves can be exploited to good benefit with color, texture, and light, giving a wall of storage (and the rest of the room) visual definition.

Of course, there's no rule that says base cabinets have to be closed while upper cabinets have to be open. Open shelving is less expensive, and for some it's a preference: There's nothing more satisfying to book lovers than shelves of books from floor to ceiling. Conversely, a solid wall of closed cabinetry, such as the beautiful banks of drawers and doors built by Shaker communities, can be a peaceful sight for tired eyes.

▼**These glass shelves flank** a fireplace in a Seattle living room. Set into a hillside, the house has no openings on the uphill side, but large windows on the opposite, eastern side allow sunlight to reach the back wall and shine through the transparent shelves.

Thick Shelves

Thick shelves in wall units have become popular again, thanks to nostalgia for the modern design of the 1950s and '60s. The easiest way to achieve this look is by applying an edge band to the front of a thin shelf, but the illusion works only from far away. Another option is to double up layers (¾ in. thick each) of plywood or medium-density fiberboard (MDF) and finish with an edge band. However, a far lighter and more stable shelf can be built by layering rows of narrow wood blocks and attaching them to thin plywood panels (top and bottom). Another way to create thick shelves is by copying the construction of a hollow-core door in which a skin of thin plywood or MDF is affixed to a beehive-type inner core—when painted or veneered, the shelves appear to be solid.

▲This thick, opaque wall in a contemporary glass house is a study in contrasts. The focus of the wall is a symmetrical arrangement of extra-thick, open shelves bordering two solid-panel cabinets that appear to float above the ground. The entertainment center is housed in the closed cabinets.

▲A family living space can't ask for more than what this good-looking, built-in wall provides. Drawers, cabinets, and closet space handle a range of items, from extra blankets to games, books, and electronic media. To maintain a traditional look, doors and drawers are inset with black iron hardware.

Staircase Storage

If there's a staircase in or adjacent to your living space, it can be the starting point (perhaps with a few modifications) for a built-in storage unit. A stair can be a dramatic focus for storage niches that are either built into the actual structure of the staircase or spun off from landings and railings. Benches with hinged or sliding lids can be incorporated into the staircase, creating a perfect storage space for bulky

▼A staircase descending from the living room is lined with a wall of adjustable shelves, creating cubbies for books in all sizes and shapes, as well as a point of visual interest.

▲This great room borrows space from a fat staircase wall for storing games and other living-space necessities next to the fireplace. A column of shelves across the hall showcases a collection of cookie jars.

▲**Both sides of this open stair are faced with** bookshelves that double as display space. Light fixture "boxes" run up the front side of the stair in between the graduated shelves. An end table is nestled between couch and cabinet where it's protected from traffic and can safely hold a sculpture.

▲**Space between studs in** this wood-on-wood staircase makes room for a collection of small objects that remind the owners of the beach.

items, such as blankets, pillows, and linens, or seasonal clothing and outerwear. Smaller box units can organize and hide board games, video games, and preschooler toys. If room allows, each family member could have a bin, drawer, or cabinet for miscellaneous stuff. Recessed or projected shelves can be used as a backup bookcase, or they can be used as display areas for photographs or artful collections. It's important to remember, however, that the stair's primary function is as a pathway to and from other floors, so storage should not disrupt traffic, and potential fire hazards, like old newspapers, should not be stored in or around the staircase.

The Entertainment Center

The prime attraction in many of today's living spaces plays an ambivalent role: We'd like to have our TV and hide it, too. Some of us remember when televisions were freestanding furniture, as was audio equipment, but today's sensibilities generally require that the television and sound system reside behind closed doors when not in use. The home for electronics is often a single wall of cabinetry that is designated the entertainment center. But as electronics evolve, so do storage options.

▼The familiar pattern of open shelving over closed cabinets flanks a distinctive, curved cabinet that conceals the entertainment center. Shelves are lit by flexible tube lighting hidden behind the frame. To open, the tall, curved doors slide behind the side panels.

◄**This wall with storage** niches is angled slightly, making it more comfortable to watch TV. The angle also separates it slightly from the fireplace, which creates balance and prevents this busy wall from being overpowering. The deep mantel molding extends into the angled portion of the wall, however, which makes the transition from fireplace to storage fluid and natural.

The Television

In most cases, the television sits in a closed cabinet, whether freestanding or built-in, outfitted with doors that won't obscure viewing when opened. A more expensive assembly involves hardware that allows the TV to be pulled out of the cabinet and swiveled so that it can be viewed from different angles. For considerable cost, a system can be designed whereby the television ascends through the top of a cabinet by way of an automated scissor- or rack-and-pinion lift; incredibly, these systems can be custom-made to accommodate a television up to 20 ft. wide. And the latest wonder of electronic evolution, the flat-screen TV, fits tight against, or even flush with, the wall. It, too, can be hidden behind doors or a painting that glides out of the way by remote control. If an all-out home theater is in your future, hire a professional consultant to devise and install the storage system; the sensitive (and multitudinous) equipment requires special consideration.

▲**This family room stores its television behind** flipper doors that require little clearance inside the cabinet because they have no hardware, only half-circle finger pulls. The television can slide almost completely out on a heavy-duty shelf, then swivel to suit various seating arrangements. A cubby attached to the top of the cabinet provides storage for additional electronic units, while a bottom cabinet holds tapes, CDs, and DVDs.

◄**Fixed, open shelves and** solid-panel doors store a lively mix of media, including books, a television, and a sound system (hidden behind the door at right). The door at left conceals a collection of videos.

▲**This flat-screen television** poses as a framed picture, hanging over the living room's centerpiece, a Japanese-style freestanding cabinet, which has plenty of nooks for videotapes and a VCR.

The Sound System

Another component that's good to hear but not necessarily see is audio equipment—call it a sound system, stereo, or hi-fi, depending on your generation. Sound systems have changed in heft and style many times over the years, but it's still the speakers that are the hardest element to store. The cleanest option is to build speakers into a wall or cabinetry; the less expensive option is simply to position them on a shelf. Audio speakers vary in requirements, but generally speaking, it's best to position them equidistant from listeners but not to center them vertically between ceiling and floor. Home-theater speakers must be placed properly to produce their full effect, so unless you have experience with acoustics, it's best to let an expert set them up. If possible, consult with the expert before you design storage for the system or you may end up backtracking to accommodate its special needs.

Measure, Measure, Measure

Proper dimensions are critical when storing electronic equipment in cabinetry. It can't be reiterated enough: Measure equipment before designing or purchasing cabinetry unless you're willing to risk buying a smaller unit than you actually need. Manufacturers' specifications should be accurate, but they frequently don't include wiring run outs—where wiring exits a unit and how much it can bend. And since models can change quickly, specs may be outdated.

In an ideal world, electronic equipment will be on hand before cabinetry is designed or purchased. It's important to consider how and where cords attach, and how much extra space will be needed for safe wiring. An electrician may demand—rightfully—as much as 6 in. between the back of the electronic component and the back of the storage unit to handle wiring. It's also important to consider all the existing appendages that must be accommodated, as well as extra space for growing collections and additional components that may be purchased down the road.

Take into account how the storage unit's doors will operate—they may require additional clearance. Flipper doors need room to slide between television and case, and pocket and sliding doors need extra room to clear the front of the television. Certain hardware, like concealed hinges, reduces side clearance.

All the Accessories

A major task of an entertainment center is to accommodate a supporting cast of multimedia: videotapes, CDs, and DVDs. Fortunately, there's a growing legion of systems customized to store specific types of multimedia. You'll find vertical and horizontal racks, covered boxes, slide-out drawers, and automated storage gadgets as simple or complex as you like. And even if it wasn't specifically designed to do so, any unit with drawers that are at least 5 in. deep can accommodate spine-up CDs or videos (just beware of extra-wide video cases). The drawer can also be fitted with 5-in.-wide slots, which will further ensure that CDs and videos stay put—assuming everyone cooperates by returning items to their proper slots. Remember to designate a specific spot— be it a drawer, nook, or slot—for remote-control devices near the appropriate equipment, or store them in a basket or other container next to seating areas.

▲ This Japanese-inspired cabinetry not only handles the television and sound system—aside from the giant speakers—it also offers plenty of options for accessory storage in drawers or bottom cupboards.

Tips for Storing Electronics

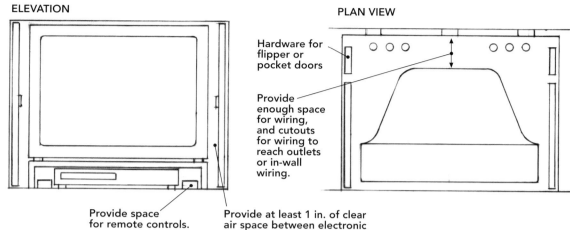

ELEVATION

PLAN VIEW

In the case of flipper doors, shelving for electronic equipment can be attached to bottom or top shelf.

Ventilation:
- In built-in cabinetry, provide cutouts in shelves and out the top or sides of cabinet to create a chimney effect.
- In freestanding cabinetry, provide cutouts in back of cabinetry.

Hardware for flipper or pocket doors

Provide enough space for wiring, and cutouts for wiring to reach outlets or in-wall wiring.

Provide space for remote controls.

Provide at least 1 in. of clear air space between electronic equipment and sides of cabinets.

◀**This entertainment center** was designed and built by a seasoned cabinetmaker who has constructed many such assemblies. His recommended details include pocket doors that slide inside the cabinet, a hanging shelf for VCR, sufficient space on the side for a sound system, and drawers for CDs and videotapes.

Options for Entertainment-Center Doors

SLIDING DOORS

A 2-in. to 6-in. clearance radius is required for the door to curve comfortably, which affects sizing.

Sliding doors slide on a track and are stored one behind the other. Extension and swivel hardware brings a television out for better viewing.

TAMBOUR DOORS

A wide cabinet can be better served by two tambour doors that slide horizontally.

Wood slats are fitted together and glued to a canvas backing. The assembly slides on a grooved track and stores out of the way.

FLIPPER AND POCKET DOORS

Flipper door hardware takes up space at the side and back of the cabinet. Size cabinets and electronics to fit.

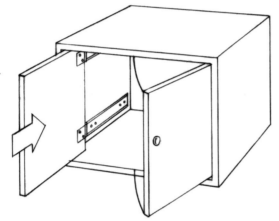

A pocket door (not shown) slides between the cabinet side and a fixed panel that conceals hardware.

A flipper door swings open, then slides back into the cabinet.

Options for Entertainment Center Doors

Swinging doors are the standard on cabinets, but there are other types of doors to consider for entertainment centers.

Sliding doors have been a rarity since the 1960s, but with modern design back in vogue, we're seeing more of them again. They're ideal for concealing televisions in more traditional-style cabinets, too. Sliding doors require no clearance in front of the cabinet (you won't bang your head on them), but they also don't allow the entire cabinet to be viewed, so television size should be planned accordingly.

Flipper and pocket doors swing open just like a swinging door, but then they slide into the cabinet along the sides (overhead flipper doors are available, too). A pocket door

◀▲**A stair landing provides an ideal, if unusual, space for a small entertainment center.** This frameless cabinet with flipper doors houses a television and an audio system, while the drawers below hold videos, DVDs, and CDs.

Breathing Room

While today's electronics don't have vacuum tubes, which were notorious for high temperatures, they still give off heat. If not properly ventilated, the heat can burn out electronic equipment prematurely. A built-in entertainment center should include enough clearance around the television or sound system for heat to dissipate, and a freestanding unit should have space behind it for ventilation. An electronics expert can provide valuable advice for your specific system.

slides between the cabinet case and a panel that hides the sliding mechanism and provides a surface for supporting shelves (see the drawing on the facing page). A flipper door slides back and hides the hardware, but it can't support shelves, of course. Ideally, each type of door retracts completely into the cabinet (the handle has to fit inside the cabinet, too) so that the doors don't obscure your view of the television inside. Be aware that flipper and pocket doors require extra depth and width to handle the hardware and the door. The pocket door takes up more space because of the extra side panel.

Tambour doors are made up of thin strips of material that slide up and out of the way on a track. They do take up space at the top of the cabinet, both for the door and the curved track, so it's necessary to allow extra clearance when sizing electronic equipment.

Fireplaces

Fireplaces have been the focus of living spaces for thousands of years (in fact, *focus* is Latin for fireplace), but even in today's more elaborate rooms, they still make an ideal focal point, exuding warmth and comfort.

Fireplaces frequently incorporate storage space for firewood, whether in a built-in niche or a movable log rack, which adds a homey ambience, but it can feature storage for other items, too. Fireplace tools are a natural addition, and the fireplace can even provide a structure for built-ins. Lidded-boxes can be installed on either side of the hearth or a bank of cabinets can become an extension of the mantel.

▼ **This sitting room is made** comfortable and peaceful by a fireplace that anchors a wealth of built-in storage. The walls of rich cherry cabinetry conceal electronic equipment, while open shelves show off an elegant book collection to best advantage—no paperback novels here.

◀**An inglenook with built-in** seating and storage cabinetry makes a cozy focus for a living room.

▲**An Arts and Crafts fireplace mantel provides** storage/display space for a favorite collection. The stone hearth holds antique tools and a basket for kindling storage. The intricate, paint-grade trim fireplace details were rendered from poplar frames and medium-density fiber-board panels.

◀**This sitting area is part** of a great room that includes dining and kitchen areas. A fireplace with rustic wood mantel is flanked by a recess for firewood and cupboards for games and such.

The mantel is a favored spot for displaying treasured pos-sessions and art. We put things on our mantels without a second thought—photos, candlesticks, art, and pottery—but consideration should be given to this potentially hot and sooty environment if the fireplace is used frequently. A fine painting or photograph can be damaged if habitually ex-posed to heat.

Showcasing Art
and Treasures

In a living space, storage plays a supporting role to aesthetics. Much of what you're storing is items that have no other purpose than beauty, and they need a protected but well-lit space where they can shine. Storage spaces as small as a wall sconce and as large as an entire wall can showcase objects in the manner that suits them best.

When planning the arrangement of artful items, it's important to remember that a living space needs a focal point

◄**There's no space untouched** by art in this Mexican-inspired house, from floor to ceiling, table to mantel. Even the architecture is art, with color and geometry balanced by sculpture, painting, and artifacts. Decorative objects are stored on ledges around the fireplace and on shelves in a range of shapes, sizes, and materials. Closed storage is provided by streamlined cabinets in a variety of harmoniously contrasting woods.

Lighting Art and Collections

Properly lighting collections is almost as important as choosing the proper display area for them. Downlights that are recessed into the ceiling or a soffit can handle several tasks. Adjustable fixtures can highlight art or be used for reading, while wall washers can be used to cast an ambient light on shelves and walls. Displays can also be lit with under-shelf, low-voltage puck lighting or with strings of incandescent bulbs, which are hidden along the top or sides of a cabinet opening. Under-shelf lighting should be positioned close to the front of the shelf, which conceals the fixture and allows light to fall on the front of highlighted objects. Side lighting is ideal for glassware and collections of arts and crafts.

▲ **This room proves that storage doesn't have** to be formal to be visually appealing and functional. Here, three bold rows of storage and display are created, beginning with the plate rail, descending to the wainscoting rail, and landing on the floor where art and book stacks lean against the wall. This casual but carefully assembled arrangement lends an intimate, personal feel to this living space without suggesting clutter or chaos.

to give the room an anchor; what that anchor is depends on personal preference, style, and habits. For avid art collectors, a prominently displayed painting gives a living space personality while reflecting that of the inhabitants. In more casual settings, an attractively housed television makes a practical and perfectly appropriate focal point.

Whatever you choose to display and no matter how you choose to display it, the important thing is to make sure that it brings you joy and makes your home a happier place to live in.

Storage as Sculpture

In many cases, the furniture that displays art can be a work of art in its own right. For instance, an antique cabinet, custom-made shelves, or niches recessed into a thick wall can become part of the display themselves, sometimes stealing the show. If that doesn't suit your style, just be sure to match the quality of the display with the storage piece, so that each balances and complements the other.

▲These alcoves turn the entire wall into a work of art within which dwell smaller pieces of folk art from around the world.

◀These cantilevered shelves create a minimalist's storage system.

Keeping Breakables Secure

Residents of earthquake-prone areas aren't the only ones who should take extra measures to secure valuable art, collections, and even electronic equipment. A household with kids or pets, an apartment in the city, or a house near an active railroad or airport will also benefit from actively securing breakables. Secure large pieces of art and electronics with straps; secure smaller pieces to shelves with a substance called earthquake putty, or museum wax, an inexpensive substance that can be removed and reused. It comes in putty form or in a clear gel that's appropriate for glass shelves. Shelves can also be covered with rubber shelf liners to keep items from slipping.

▲In this sitting loft, which perches over the living room, a stunning collection of pottery is displayed in specially designed niches.

12

Work-Space Storage

►**A designer thrives in this** lively but orderly work space, thanks to a modular desk outfitted with adjustable shelves of varying depths. The ribbon board to the left stores inspirational images in the open for easy access.

H ome is not the sanctuary that it once was, and there's no longer a distinct boundary between our home lives and our work lives. For an increasing number of people, home and office are one and the same, and even if not, it's a rare family these days that doesn't bring work home—be it overtime work for a deadline, freelance projects on the side, or for the kids, good old-fashioned homework. With this in mind, it's important to try to minimize the feeling that we're at work even when we're at home. While it can't keep you from being a workaholic, a proper work-space setup can help prevent the paraphernalia of work from invading the rest of your living space, and it will help you stay focused when work is necessary.

Since work spaces almost always include a computer these days, they aren't just about drudgery anymore; surfing the Web has become a national pastime, while computer games are a childhood (and sometimes adulthood) staple. Many people are now more sophisticated in their approach to running a household as well and may use a computer for taxes, bills, shopping, and even home-improvement projects. With all this activity centered around the computer, it's wise to not just plop the thing down anywhere you see a flat surface.

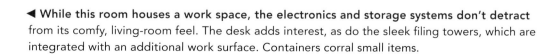

◄ **While this room houses a work space, the electronics and storage systems don't detract** from its comfy, living-room feel. The desk adds interest, as do the sleek filing towers, which are integrated with an additional work surface. Containers corral small items.

Make Room
for a Home Office

It's a matter of degrees when it comes to the difference between office storage for a home business and office storage for people who bring some work home. Each setting will need to include storage for a computer and all of its electronic peripherals, plus storage for office supplies. But the peripherals for a home business will likely be bigger, more expensive, require more space, and be used more frequently, making it essential to keep all equipment easily accessible. The components of an occasional office can be stored away into pockets of space and pulled out when needed. Ideally, either setup will have its own room, but with efficient storage, the occasional office can find a home in a shared room. While it may be ideal for a home office to have a room of its own, budget and space constraints often call for a home office to fit within the fabric of a shared

◄▲ **Sometimes a home office has to find** room anywhere it can; here, it's under the eaves of a Craftsman-style addition. The architect/ owner tucks books into freestanding bookcases and a built-in oak wall cabinet, but he also depends on overflow book storage in the hallway. The wall cabinet has a couple of handy details, including adjustable shelves and a slot for blueprints.

◀This office nook is tucked between the kitchen and dining areas in a house for a big family in Jackson, Wyoming. Storage is handled by built-in file and supply drawers, along with built-in shelves. The shelves are varying shapes and sizes, which allows for the most versatile storage, accommodating everything from paper clips to a miniature library. The half wall separates this work space without closing off the small room.

▶Rather than close off a study with walls, these homeowners chose to preserve free-flowing space while still incorporating certain necessities. A freestanding bookcase is tucked into a well-lit niche and accompanied by an unfussy table and chair; the ensemble creates a work area without taking up extra room or getting bogged down in work space extras that these homeowners didn't need. The sleek, double-door closets across the hall handle any unsightly storage or clutter.

When All Else Fails...

If there's no space to borrow in the usual rooms, search for less obvious pockets of space, such as a walk-in closet, an alcove under a staircase, the corner of a hallway, or on a stair landing—even a standard 2-ft. closet can become a makeshift office, albeit a tight one. Don't ignore looks or function when setting up this captured space, however; attractive shelves are easy to find, and institutional desks or filing cabinets can be refurbished to complement the surrounding space.

room. This can make functional storage tricky due to limited space and aesthetics.

After you've selected a room (keep in mind how you'll use the space and how that will affect other household activities), think about how you can best supply storage without disrupting the room's flow and style. For instance, an antique desk or table that's refitted to accommodate modern computer equipment may be a better option for a traditional living room than a sleek, modern computer desk. Make peripheral equipment easy to conceal—in drawers, on carts, behind doors—not only to maintain appearances for guests and family but also to protect work from family and guests.

Capturing Storage Space

Instead of fighting small or odd-shaped spaces, modify storage for a custom fit. Think broadly about the size and shape of the items you need to store and map out the space you have to work with, including all those scraps of wasted space that seem useless. With a little ingenuity, you'll probably find that you have more storage space than you originally thought.

A WORK SPACE UNDER THE EAVES

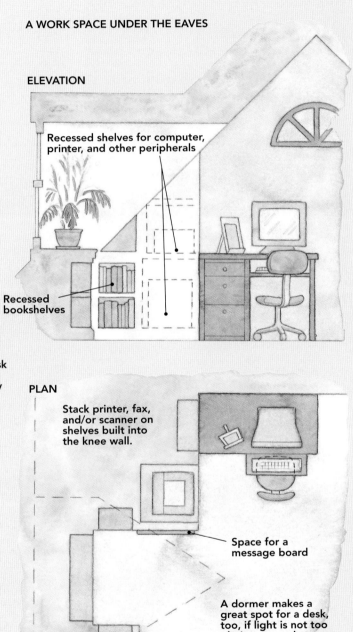

ELEVATION

Recessed shelves for computer, printer, and other peripherals

Recessed bookshelves

PLAN

Stack printer, fax, and/or scanner on shelves built into the knee wall.

Space for a message board

A dormer makes a great spot for a desk, too, if light is not too glaring or can be shaded.

Fit bookshelves into knee wall. A dormer offers extra space for recessed shelving or drawers.

A WORK SPACE UNDER A STAIR

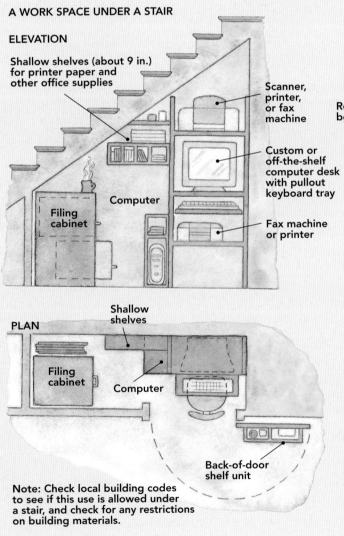

ELEVATION

Shallow shelves (about 9 in.) for printer paper and other office supplies

Scanner, printer, or fax machine

Custom or off-the-shelf computer desk with pullout keyboard tray

Fax machine or printer

Filing cabinet

Computer

PLAN

Shallow shelves

Filing cabinet

Computer

Back-of-door shelf unit

Note: Check local building codes to see if this use is allowed under a stair, and check for any restrictions on building materials.

The Work-Space Desk

M ost families have at least one computer in their house, and many have several. The most minimal setup is a chair and a table for a laptop computer—or just a chair and a lap. But add on a printer, a fax machine, and perhaps even a scanner, and you realize that gone are the days when a simple desk would do. With all that equipment vying for space on the desktop, we forget that we need some space for spreading out books and papers, too. It's also necessary to consider drawer space for files, peripherals, and traditional stationery supplies. An L-shaped configuration is superior to a straight run because it provides space for a computer as well as open, flat space for additional storage, peripheral equipment, or supplies, or that can be used for noncomputer work; a

▲1915 Prairie-style home was updated with this study and computer alcove rendered in quartersawn white oak. Of course, there is no computer desk precedent in Prairie-style design, but the woodwork itself takes on the molding and proportions of the Prairie style and keeps these modern necessities from feeling too out of place.

▲Work is a family affair in this office, which houses two architects (father and son) and an interior designer (mom). For this expansive home office, located in a long hallway between bedrooms, maple cabinets and open shelving accommodate immense storage needs, from books to product manuals to paperwork. Opposite, a work surface is punctuated by vertical shelves and cubbies for blueprints and drafting supplies.

alcove situated off the living area of this long, opened room. A wall-height window frames a breathtaking view, so why interrupt it with a desk? Instead, a streamlined work surface is provided by a thick glass shelf. The bookcase has adjustable shelves (with edge bands) that tuck in behind a face frame and provide open and closed storage for books, office supplies, and computer peripherals.

U-shaped layout offers even more space within easy reach. These extra legs of desk space can be simple tabletops, or they can be fitted with drawers and cabinets, depending on how much storage you need.

Built-in desks that are custom-made to suit your specific storage requirements are a plus, but there's a wide selection of self-contained workstations available online and in stores and catalogs. The handy homeowner may elect to save money and buy knocked down (KD) or ready-to-assemble (RTA) workstations, available in a variety of materials and styles. Shop carefully for these systems, however, as quality and price vary, as does the time it takes to assemble them—from a couple of hours to a couple of days if a part is missing.

Paper and Paperwork

Unless you have the luxury of endless space and can store everything close by, office-supply and paperwork storage will be most efficient if it corresponds to frequency of use. Keep the stuff that you constantly need nearby and get everything else off the desktop.

Objects needed for work—pens, paper clips, sticky pads, tape, rubber bands, a stapler—should be kept in a consistent place, and subdivided storage is a must whether it's cubbyholes, jars, or a shallow drawer with dividers.

Large stacks of paper should be separated by type and stored flat in a dust-free environment, such as on shelves in wall and base cabinets or on pullout trays. Envelopes of various sizes and types are best stored in slots that allow for quick retrieval.

Paperwork can foil even the best laid storage plans—it threatens to overrun our lives every time the mail comes. Paperwork that requires storage—letters, product information, contracts, and so forth—should never be stored in desktop stacks for any length of time because they clutter a work space and will get ruined or lost. Only paperwork that needs immediate attention should be stored on the desktop, and it should be kept in labeled trays, if possible.

Paperwork that needs to be kept for future reference should be stored in active files, preferably in file folders that are stored vertically. Hanging files can then be stored in cardboard storage boxes, free-standing file cabinets, or file drawers built into the work-space desk. The same rule that applies to office supplies applies to files—figure out what you need regularly and use prime real estate for that paperwork. Everything else can be put wherever you have room, even if it's in another room. And although it takes discipline, periodically purging active files is essential for keeping your home-office storage running smoothly.

▲ **Twenty-first-century computer equipment** fits on an antique desk in this well-designed home office, while the hutch provides four file drawers in the base cabinet along with fixed, open shelves of various sizes for convenient and diverse storage.

Upgrading Old Furniture for the Computer Age

An antique desk may be the best aesthetic solution for a computer in a traditional space, but using the computer for long periods at an old desk can be a pain—literally. The surface will likely be too high for comfortable keyboarding. If the desk apron is not too deep and a drawer doesn't intervene, a taller seat may do the trick, along with a footstool for comfort; if that doesn't work and you have your heart set on the piece, a furniture restorer may be able to modify the desk, but that may sacrifice its integrity and/or value. If the desk is a valuable antique, you may also want to reconsider drilling holes to channel wiring; a fully charged laptop may be a better companion to antiquity.

▲ **A family study shows that elegance and plastic toys** can coexist in peace. This large freestanding desk-cum-bookcase is designed to look antique, with built-in cubbies and slots, but it's built for the digital present with space for a monitor, keyboard tray, and drawers for printer and fax machines. A satellite desk provides space for serious work by kids of all ages.

Measure for Size and Comfort

To gauge how much storage space a desktop will provide—and how much additional storage you'll need for peripherals and other supplies—it's important to first determine how much room the monitor and computer will need. Make sure the desk you select is deep enough to position the monitor so that it's at least 18 in. away from your eyes. A standard-sized monitor needs a 24-in.-deep space. A pullout or fixed keyboard tray that sits below the desktop will help conserve desktop space while helping to achieve proper ergonomics (arms should rest at a comfortable 90° angle with wrists straight or angled slightly downward). It's preferable to choose a keyboard that different users can adjust and that is wide enough for both a keyboard and a mouse.

► **In this attractive but serious-minded study,** storage is handled by a built-in wall unit with a freestanding base cabinet and desk below. Note that the desk swells out as it approaches the window so that the keyboard tray and monitor can tilt away from window glare. The wall unit has cubby drawers, perfect for sorting mail or bills. The base cabinet offers drawers in a variety of sizes, ensuring that all manner of items can be accommodated.

▲ **A computer requires a lot of support.** This one has a keyboard that slides into a slot under the monitor, a fax machine/copier on the side of the monitor (where it's immediately handy for receiving faxes any time of day or night), and a printer on a roll-out shelf, so that it can be turned off and tucked away when office hours are over. The printer is plugged into a receptacle that's installed inside the cabinet itself. The CPU sits under the drawer to the far right. The slim drawer under the monitor contains pencils, paper clips, and similar office supplies.

What to Do with Peripherals

Peripherals, the electronic devices that connect to the computer, can overwhelm a work space. Just tick off those you have (or want): printer, fax machine, scanner, mouse, keyboard, modem, digital camera, personal digital assistant (PDA), and the list grows daily as new devices are born. Make room for peripherals in order of their use. A printer is likely high on that list, so keep it on the desktop or reasonably close by. If space is at a premium, store it in the closest dust-free environment (a desk drawer, nearby closet, pullout shelf), but try to avoid storing it under the desk unless you vacuum daily and enjoy crawling around on the floor. A fax machine is probably used far less often, so it can be stored farther down the line—even in another room. If you use a scanner or copier frequently, place it on the desktop on the side opposite your mouse hand, or on a desktop surface perpendicular to the monitor but still comfortably close.

Home Library

Bookshelves are a necessity in a work space, but a work space is not necessary to justify bookshelves. Whether work space and library are combined or separate will dictate what kind of library you have, from a few cantilevered shelves to an entire room outfitted with baronial built-ins. Regardless, every house needs some kind of storage space for books.

Built-in bookshelf cabinetry can give a room character and provide a sense of depth. Recessing built-ins into the wall space is a more economical use of space, and makes a room appear larger.

Freestanding bookshelves can appear nearly as substantial as built-in cabinetry, and they offer several advantages over built-ins. They're much more affordable,

▲This study features built-in bookshelves recessed into brick walls. The case and shelves are oak veneer, and shelves are thickened with an edge band. Although they are aligned, the shelves are adjustable—just in case.

they can be used to subdivide a room or screen one area from another, and they're also mobile. Modular freestanding units are generally even more affordable, and they can be custom selected to suit your specific collection; they can also be reassembled to fit changing needs.

Regardless of the bookcases you choose, there are few things to keep in mind about shelves:

While paperbacks can fit on much shallower shelves, 10-in.- to 11-in.-deep shelves will house most hardcover books and still leave a bit of shelf exposed in front; this is

a much neater look than books that overhang. Should shelves be fixed or adjustable? Opinions vary, but if your collection is just starting out, adjustable shelving will give you far more storage flexibility.

▲ A frequent design mistake is to situate shelving too low over a chair or couch, making it difficult to sit comfortably. This bookcase bypasses that problem (without sacrificing storage space) with its graduated-depth shelves. Shallow lower shelves are the perfect depth for family photos, while upper shelves hold books of various sizes.

Secret Compartments

You've seen books that have been hollowed out for jewel stashing, but here are some less-clichéd places in a library or study:

- The top of a bookshelf can be fitted with a false top that's hidden behind molding.
- Cabinet drawers can be fitted with false bottoms that slide in and out of place.
- The top few inches of a railing post can be drilled out and covered with a post cap.
- Tables can be fitted with hidden drawers that drop open when unbolted.
- Finally, there is the cinematically inspired bookcase that swings open to reveal a whole secret room—your kids will love it.

13

Bedrooms and Closets

Of all the rooms in a house, the bedroom has the potential for the most eclectic assortment of storage. In a smaller house, the bedroom might contain the only available space for a desk and computer, while the ideal master bedroom in a big house may call for an entertainment center and have a suite of rooms attached. Whatever extras you have in a bedroom, it's clothing that annexes most of the storage space, even if you're lucky enough to have this space in an adjacent dressing room or walk-in closet. In fact, most bedroom storage is found behind closed doors, from wall closets to full-blown dressing suites, supplemented by chests of drawers or built-in cabinetry. The balance of bedroom storage is devoted to the things you need for sleeping and waking, such as a stack of books and an alarm clock, and to the creature comforts that you choose to surround yourself with.

►**Well-designed closet** storage, like the system shown here, offers a combination of rods and shelves, which ensures that each piece of clothing can be stored in the manner that suits it best.

◄**This unique unit offers bed, headboard, storage, and display all in one. Multiple levels** of storage are devised with drawers of various sizes, and hidden cabinets make use of the back side of the unit without disrupting its sleek look. For these committed in-bed readers, light fixtures built into the headboard are a blessing. The unit also functions as a partition, subdividing and defining this spacious room.

Where to Store Clothes

Like the kitchen pantry with its 10 brands each of cereal, cookies, and soup, today's closet has to handle a colossal variety of clothing, most of which our ancestors never dreamed of; we have far more specialized clothes than some earlier generations—just compare your wardrobe with that of your great-grandmother. You may wear stretchy, space-age gear for biking, white togs for tennis, overalls for gardening, casual clothes for home, different casual clothes for going out, skirt and pantsuits for work, elegant clothes for

▲This built-in bureau is integrated with the room's architecture and paneling, creating both a beautiful composition and an abundance of storage.

▲ **A skylight that creates headroom and light** in this closet also makes the perfect niche for a built-in bureau. Clothes hang in easy reach on either side.

▲ **A treasured family heirloom, this antique** tansu chest has a highly visible but out-of-the-way spot nestled in a recessed niche near the entryway to the master bedroom suite. Its variety of drawers and cabinets handle an array of storage needs.

evening, and lounging wear for various seasons—not to mention the many accessories that go with them.

Keeping clothes orderly and accessible is no minor task. The traditional chest of drawers or an armoire is a start but rarely provides adequate storage. However, freestanding cabinetry can add much to a bedroom's ambience, so it should be selected with an eye toward aesthetics as well as function. Freestanding furniture is generally supplemented by a closet (if your bedroom doesn't include one, consider going to any length to create one), be it the standard 2-ft.-deep wall closet or a room-size walk-in. In either event, storage space will go a lot further if the closet is properly outfitted with well-thought-out shelving, hooks, rods, and cubbies. While internal storage systems can be custom designed, they've become widely available off-the-shelf, and you can practically buy your way to custom storage, thanks to the myriad modular units in the marketplace. In-the-closet cabinetry also has a lighter load and fewer viewers than the cabinetry in your kitchen, living room, or study, so it can be detailed more simply and focused on function rather than form. However you store your clothes, keeping them neat and accessible is the key to a good start in the morning.

Furniture for Clothes

Chest of drawers, bureau, armoire, dresser, chiffonier—whatever you call your freestanding furniture for clothing, chances are it's furnished mostly with drawers. Go for an assortment of depths, if possible, or fit it with compartments that keep items from deep tangles. Line with shelf paper or cloth to avoid staining from unfinished interiors, especially from cedar-lined drawers. Drawer storage is best for small items, such as lingerie, underwear, socks, swimsuits, exercise clothes, belts, and the like. Sweaters and knit shirts can be stored in drawers, but they are easier to see and access on fixed or pullout shelves.

▲**Storage doesn't have to be** fancy to be functional. This simple closet, concealed by a curtain rather than a door, takes care of storage necessities while adding charm and openness to a small, rustic bedroom.

▲**This is a setup photo,** of course—who has a closet that looks like this?—but it illustrates the point that different types of clothes require different types of storage. Single poles are necessary for long items, but doubling up rods makes the most efficient use of space and is acceptable for most clothes. Adjustable shelves handle a variety of needs from hats to sweaters to shoes.

Wall Closets, Shallow and Deep

The most basic of wall closets is a standard 2 ft. deep and generally contains a single shelf positioned 68 in. off the floor, along with a rod that's 1 in. to 2 in. just below the shelf; long spans will require a midspan bracket for the pole. If this arrangement suits you, count yourself lucky, but most of us could do with a little more variety—and depth. Just an extra 6 in. will allow better access to shelves installed along the side walls and more room for storage on the back of the door, which is a good place for shoe pockets, tie and belt racks, and other hanging accessories. Home-design stores and catalogs offer an array of closet systems that provide drawers, shelves, rods, and hooks that you can mix and match at will. A wall closet that's built into a wall under a gabled roof can be extended into the knee-wall space, where it's possible to hang a lower rod for out-of-season clothes.

Off-the-shelf storage systems are made in several materials, from wire to plastic to panel products (panel products include particleboard, medium-density fiberboard (MDF), plywood, and combination products). For shelves and drawers, wire systems allow clothes to breathe, but they will leave an imprint on fine knits; solid shelves are a better choice for delicate folded items.

Walk-In Closets and Dressing Rooms

A walk-in closet doesn't necessarily have the space you need to dress, so you can call a big walk-in closet a dressing room, especially if it's fitted with a dressing table and a mirror (a three-way mirror, if you have the space and the courage). If you can, design a walk-in closet to specifically

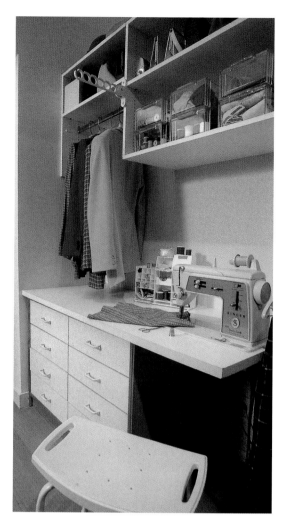

▲▶This dressing room is a clothes aficionado's dream. It has every kind of storage a couple needs, including hooks, poles, shelves, drawers, and enough room to park a car. The rods are perfectly designed for maximum efficiency, accommodating garments of any length, while the shelves are varied to hold shoes and boots of all sizes. At the far end, a sewing station resides in easy reach of clothes that need repair; the desk it sits on provides even more drawers and shelves for sewing supplies and other paraphernalia.

Safe Storage

Bedrooms often become the repository of safes. Smaller safes can be installed after the house is built, but large or built-in safes require forethought. A large safe can damage a floor as it's hauled into place, so protect floors carefully or, if you're building, plan to finish them after the safe is installed. A safe that is bolted to the floor will provide the most security from burglary, of course, but it can't be moved in case of a fire. No safe is completely fireproof, but fire-resistant safes are available. If you're building and plan to include a built-in safe, don't note its location on house plans. There's no need to spread the news around a job site, and you'll probably need to file a set of those plans with the town hall, where even more eyes would be privy to its location.

▲ **This dressing hall, situated off the bedroom,** is an elegant space, with beaded panels in flat frames along with glass hardware. The multitude of doors conceals all the shelves, closet poles, drawers, and hooks that this couple requires for clothing storage. The floor-to-ceiling window lets in lots of light and offers a relaxing view of a private garden.

suit you and your collection of clothes. Count and measure all the items you'll be keeping and build in some space for adding clothes (and shoes!). The ideal dressing room has the space to provide storage in many forms, and will provide room to change clothes easily. Include a hamper in the dressing room, as well as a trash can for the daily debris culled from pockets, a bowl for loose change, and tools for taking care of clothes, such as brushes, sewing tools, and

▲ **This handsome, built-in** cabinet efficiently houses an entire wardrobe. Shoes are kept in a pullout unit, drawers handle folded clothes and lingerie, and a single closet pole maintains hanging clothes, with hats and belts coiled or stacked on the raised cabinet floor. Off-season clothes are culled regularly and stored in hall closets outside the bedroom.

▶ **This dressing room keeps** everything in its place, with paneled doors concealing hanging clothes and plenty of drawer storage for accessories and folded clothes. A niche with mirrored sides and back provides a three-way view during dressing.

possibly an ironing board and a steamer. Of course, the dressing room should be adjacent to the master bathroom, and to the washer and dryer if your preference is to wash clothes near bedrooms and bathrooms rather than near the kitchen or in the basement.

How to Store Clothes

Whether clothes are stored in dressers, wall closets, or dressing rooms, here are some basics for organizing clothes to keep them in good shape while getting the most from the available space. The first step is to organize clothes by type; the exception is an unimpeachable ensemble, which should be stored together. Store clothes to their best advantage, keeping in mind how they are made and how you wear them. Even off-season or rarely worn clothes should be hung properly with enough room to breathe; consider installing a secondary rod rather than squashing them in with your active wardrobe. Another important step in preserving your clothes is to remove plastic dry-cleaner bags immediately and let the clothes air out for a day or two before putting them away.

Clothes to Hang

A majority of clothing is best stored hanging. But how you hang items will determine whether you have a wrinkled mess or a functional wardrobe. Taking time to measure and think out your closet needs will make a huge difference in how well your closet operates, and thus, how smooth or annoying the task of dressing is. Here are some guidelines to get you started.

Poles Dresses, blouses, shirts, coats, trousers, and skirts are best stored on hangers, so the more closet poles, the better. Short spans for each type of clothing work the best.

Hangers The right hanger goes a long way in ensuring tidy closet storage. Use tubular, plastic hangers for shirts, padded-shoulder

▼**A tidy shirt closet actually makes dry-**cleaner hangers look appealing, with shirts neatly hung on a chrome closet pole. A translucent plastic bin holds shirts ready for the cleaners. The satiny curtain door provides a rich contrast to the flat-framed cherry cabinetry, which conceals folded clothing. Cherry pullout shelves keep shoes neat and easy to access.

▼ ▶ **You have almost infinite options for** shelving heights in this dressing room, with holes for pins drilled closely together. Shelves, solid drawers, wire pullout baskets, hooks, and rods supply a multitude of storage needs. Sweaters are best folded so they won't stretch on hangers, belts are hung, socks and jammies are in pullout wire baskets, and underwear is stashed in closed drawers.

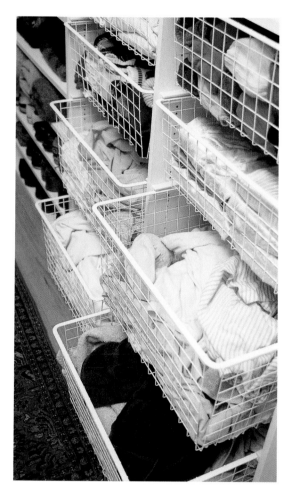

hangers for slippery blouses and delicate knits, and wood or plastic hangers with bowed backs and trouser bars for pantsuits. If you prefer to hang pants without a centerfold, use hangers with clips and adjust the height of the rod to accommodate the length of the pants—long skirts will require the same.

Pegs You won't want to store dresses, blouses, and shirts on pegs or hooks, but don't ignore these handy devices. You'll need them for robes, towels, work shirts, overalls, and possibly belts and scarves.

Clothes to Fold

It's best to fold knits rather than hang them, but some sweaters can be folded and hung on the bar of a hanger, preferably a thick one with a nonslip surface. Adjustable shelves will allow for customized spacing, but be sure to order enough; it's better to space shelves closely for folded items—a sky-high stack of sweaters is not only unwieldy, but it makes for more wrinkles and less ventilation. Keep like items stored together, even if it means only one item per stack; this will prevent you from rummaging through multiple shelves and messing up all the piles.

Finding Storage Pockets

The bedroom is personal, private space, and carving out storage from corners, eaves, and walls provides a wonderful opportunity to add charm and coziness to the room. Because many bedrooms are located on the top floor, it's often possible to make use of roof shapes for captured storage space, whether in a knee wall or in the interesting thickened walls made by dormers that intersect gabled roofs. Built-in drawers or closets can make use of space that is otherwise wasted, and designing storage in this way customizes it to your specific needs, while adding a unique and interesting touch to your bedroom.

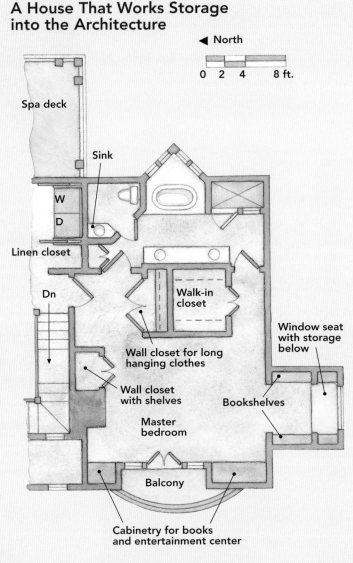

A House That Works Storage into the Architecture

◀ North

0 2 4 8 ft.

Spa deck

Sink

W

D

Linen closet

Dn

Walk-in closet

Window seat with storage below

Wall closet for long hanging clothes

Wall closet with shelves

Bookshelves

Master bedroom

Balcony

Cabinetry for books and entertainment center

▲This master bedroom uses intersecting roof lines to create interesting storage opportunities. A bookshelf is built into the dormer wall, and two built-in cabinets flank the balcony doors; the one to the left contains a television and audio system.

Fit Storage under the Eaves

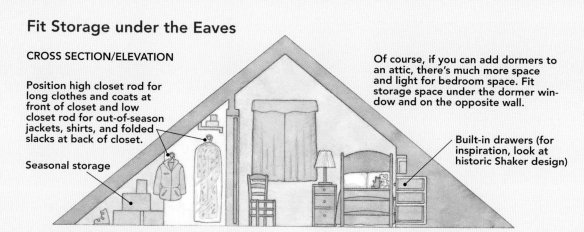

CROSS SECTION/ELEVATION

Position high closet rod for long clothes and coats at front of closet and low closet rod for out-of-season jackets, shirts, and folded slacks at back of closet.

Seasonal storage

Of course, if you can add dormers to an attic, there's much more space and light for bedroom space. Fit storage space under the dormer window and on the opposite wall.

Built-in drawers (for inspiration, look at historic Shaker design)

FLOOR PLAN

Back of closet, under eaves, tends to be warmer or cooler than the rest of the attic, but it's suitable for seasonal storage such as ski clothes and holiday decorations.

Don't fill the gable-end wall with too much storage. Use that brighter space for a desk or bed, and push closets to the center of the attic.

To keep a space under a gable roof from looking less like an attic, build knee walls where the ceiling reaches about 4 ft.—where it's comfortable to reach, if not stand. Recess bookcase space, drawer space, and closets into knee-wall cavities.

Low rod for out-of-season short clothes

High rod for longer clothes

◀The dormer in this small room (far left) creates space for a window seat with storage, while lending visual interest and an expanded sense of height and depth. Although this room is only 11 ft. by 15 ft.—small for today's master bedrooms—it feels ample and elegant.

◀The baby's room has the same dormer configuration as the master bedroom, but the corners are left open with shelves for toys.

◄**A bamboo ladder leaning** against the wall makes an attractive and handy rack for ties and belts.

Wire shelving will make marks on sweaters and fine knits, but they're a boon for shoes, hats, and other items that benefit from a good airing. If your shelving is built-in and will be finished on site, take heed of the tip offered for shelving in pantries and give closet woodwork a glossy or satin finish, and allow finishes to dry completely.

Storing Accessories

Accessories can take over a closet, so it makes sense to dedicate space to storing them efficiently. There's no shortage of closet accessories that store accessories, but to figure out exactly what you need, you may want to take a field trip to your favorite clothing store and learn from the way they store accessories; if they're doing it right, everything should be easy to access and just as easy to put back.

Ties   The best tie-storage methods keep all ties easy to see and get to, which means not on a tie hanger that's tucked between shirts. Fine men's-clothing stores always store ties flat so that ties, which are bias-cut, won't stretch. This method is harder to accomplish at home, but if there's

▲**Anyone who loves shoes—but hates the** tangled mess they make on the floor—would love a closet like this, with adjustable shelves that offer many rows to neatly fit many shoes.

His-and-Her Closets

In this Martha's Vineyard house, the master bedroom suite contains his-and-her dressing rooms that have the same basic design but different arrangements. Each has built-in drawers, a bench, and closet rods of varying heights. Drawers have scooped-out pulls for easy opening. To give the closets a more spacious feel and to maximize natural light from the skylight, the walls are stopped short of the ceiling; the resulting boxes are trimmed with molding and Craftsman-style brackets. A chest, which was custom-built for the room along with the bed, holds blankets and extra bed linens.

All the furniture and trim is built from reclaimed cypress, which designer South Mountain Company calls its "bread-and-butter" wood. Reclaimed cypress is timber that sank to river bottoms when old-growth cypress forests were heavily logged a century ago. This dense wood has lots of warmth and character and is easy to work into furniture and molding. The floor is reclaimed pine.

▲▶The two closet boxes are stopped short of the ceiling to take advantage of natural light. Positioning the closets at the entry to the bedroom makes for a more private entrance into the room. The couple's joint study is beyond the bed.

▲ **In this bedroom, a sloped** roof with a dormer makes a cozy window seat that also provides storage for off-season clothes. The seat has hinged panels that allow for easy access.

enough space, ties can be folded and stored in shallow drawers or on pullout shelves. Hanging ties over pegs on a wall rack is a happy compromise.

Shoes Shoes are best stored off the floor on eye-level shelves or in pull-out units, where they won't be kicked around and separated from their mates. If shoes have to stay at floor level, consider an adjustable shoe rack that will stretch along the back or side wall of the closet. Otherwise, store shoes in pockets or on a shoe rack that fits on the back of the door.

▲ **This cupboard, located in a dressing room,** is designed to store shoe-shining equipment—a nice extra for the truly shoe obsessed.

Belts Belts can be coiled and stored in individual slots in a shallow cabinet or in a partitioned drawer, in clear pockets in a hanging rack, or on individual pegs on the wall. But beware of stacking belts on pegs; you'll always want the belt at the back of the stack.

Hats Fine hats must be stored under wraps in hat boxes with protective tissue and some ventilation. Caps are most easily seen and accessed if they are hung on pegs rather than set on shelves or thrown in a basket. Soft hats, such as berets, will stretch on pegs, so keep them neatly stacked on shelves.

Storing Out-of-Season Clothes

Most of us have far too many clothes to keep in active storage all year. Off-season clothes can be stored in a commodious bedroom closet, but if space is at a premium, they are perfect candidates for out-of-the-way storage niches, from the top shelf of a closet to storage drawers or boxes under beds. All clothes should be cleaned before they are put away, and boxes should be labeled so it's easier to unpack when the temperature changes. Avoid lining boxes with, or storing hanging clothes in, dry-cleaner bags, which don't let clothes breathe and may discolor delicate fabrics. If there's closet-rod space available, consider purchasing cloth or nylon garment bags for hanging storage or bags with slots for storing knits and shoes. Another option is a rolling rack fitted with a canvas tent, which protects clothes from dust and humidity; this can be rolled into a spare bedroom or even the basement or attic as long as those areas are free from dampness and vermin and have a stable temperature. Archival boxes and tissue are the best bet for long-term storage of favorite clothes that will become heirlooms. Keep all storage containers away from excessive heat and humidity.

Discouraging Moths

The first storage myth to dispel is that a cedar closet will keep moths away from woolens. It's true that cedar oil can kill young larvae, but it has not been proven to kill adult moths and eggs, and it's not known what amount of cedar oil will do the trick. Only naphthalene and paradichlorobenzene (found in mothballs) are proven to kill moths in all stages and only if not diluted by too much air circulation. But both of these chemicals are toxic (the latter is carcinogenic), and clothes stored with mothballs should be isolated from rooms where you spend time.

Consider discouraging moths from your woolens in a safer way. Moths love grease, sweat, food stains, and starch, so the very best way to prevent moth damage is to brush woolen garments after you wear them and to clean and brush all garments before putting them back on shelves, in drawers, or in chests. It's also wise to clean containers and closets before loading them up with long-term or off-season storage; also keep this long-term storage as cool and dry as possible.

Since cedar does provide some discouragement to moths, there's no harm in using it to line drawers, trunks, and closets that are used to store out-of-season wool clothing. Line cedar containers with a clean sheet or muslin before storing woolens, however, because the cedar can stain light-colored fibers.

The Bed

The bed is the centerpiece of most bedrooms, and while it can take up considerable space and require adjacent storage, it can also provide storage. Beds themselves can be stashed in unexpected places, even places other than a bedroom, or under eaves and in walls to make either a cozy space for sleeping or a space that converts by day to a window seat or retreat for quiet activities.

▲The ultimate in bedside tables is a thick wall devoted to storage. This handsome wall-cum-headboard has a multitude of drawers and a shelf for odds and ends. The remaining space in the unit is dedicated to storage that serves the master bathroom (located behind it).

◀▼**This headboard operates** as a storage unit and a room divider. On the bed side it holds books, a clock, and a phone, and on the opposite side it offers drawers for folded clothes and a cabinet with closed doors that conceal shelving.

▲**This antiqued cupboard prevents stacks of** reading material from overwhelming the bedside, and the top drawer makes a handy place to stash reading glasses and the like. A chest by the window contains blankets and extra pillows.

Bedside Storage

A bed without bedside storage is a sorry state of affairs. Where else can you deposit bedtime books and magazines, a glass of water, your watch, a pad and pencil for noting midnight inspirations, and a clock radio? The beside table is a time-honored tradition, but it's possible to provide bedside storage in other ways—by building shelves into a headboard or by tucking the bed into built-in cabinetry that contains shelves and drawers. The key to functional bedside storage is to make it easy to reach without falling out of bed, to keep open shelves away from where you will sit up in bed and lean against pillows, and to provide a light nearby that can be turned off from the bed. A lockable drawer is a handy addition if you require nighttime medications and live in a household with small children.

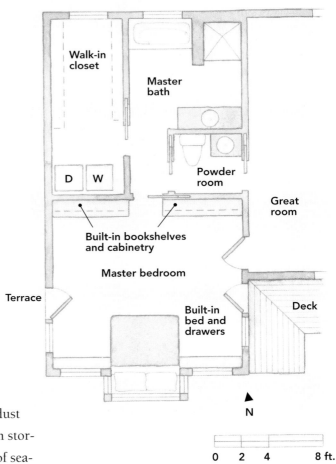

◀This master bedroom bed is built into a south-facing bump-out to take advantage of a solar alarm clock. Homeowners/newlyweds Mike Guertin (a builder) and Susan Aitcheson (an architect) designed the cabinetry to incorporate long drawers and generous surfaces for bedside storage (see the floor plan below).

A House That Maximizes Bedroom Space

Walk-in closet

Master bath

D W

Powder room

Great room

Built-in bookshelves and cabinetry

Master bedroom

Terrace

Built-in bed and drawers

Deck

N

0   2   4   8 ft.

Storage under the Bed

The space under the bed can be used for more than dust bunnies and the errant shoe. It's perfect for long-term storage of off-season clothes or linens, luggage, or even of seasonal decorations. Since a bedroom is likely to be kept at a comfortable temperature, this may be the perfect spot for storing relatively fragile items, such as archived photographs. But keep storage to a minimum of containers, such as shallow rollout bins, and try to match the bin to the space available so that there's little chance for dust to collect. An off-the-shelf bin can hide behind a dust ruffle, or drawers and rollout shelves can be built into the bed frame itself. Casters will make access much easier, and a zipper or flip top will keep dust and critters out of the contents.

▲A bed for one person needs but one bedside table. This heavy-duty, stainless-steel cabinet keeps books behind a door and bedside odds and ends in a drawer so the top can be kept relatively clear. The big leather stool officially acts as a step up to the bed, but it also provides temporary storage.

Fitting In a Fold-Down Bed

Architect Patrick Camus and his wife, Lynnette, live in a 10-ft.-wide town house that doesn't leave much room for guests, but they found a way to be hospitable by squeezing a fold-down bed into a small spare room. Patrick was not enamored of the off-the-shelf, Murphy-style bed kits that he saw, so he designed and built one to blend seamlessly into accompanying cabinetry—until guests arrive, there's no indication that a bed exists. The center section of wainscoting, which is actually a box on wheels, pulls out and acts as both footboard and storage for a comforter. The center panel is a bed frame constructed of ¾-in.-thick, 5-ft.-by-10-ft. sheets of medium-density fiberboard, which are rabbeted into a poplar frame that is the depth of a foam mattress. This bed frame is unbolted from the built-in shelves and carefully lowered to rest on the wainscoting/footboard. The head of the bed remains hinged to the wall structure.

▲This study doubles as a guest room in a small town house. When closed, the bed is completely camouflaged by the wainscoting and wall panel.

▲The wainscoting rolls away from the wall to become a footboard, then the panel is unlocked and lowered to rest on the footboard. The comforter is rolled up and stored inside and the closed cabinets that flank the bed hold pillows.

Kids' Bedroom Storage

They may be smaller than their parents, but kids often require more storage space in their bedrooms because unlike their parents, all their worldly possessions have to fit in one room. As they grow, kids' storage needs evolve, but the trick is to start low with storage and spread it out horizontally, making it easy for little kids to reach.

Provide lots of open shelving, and outfit the shelves with removable, shallow boxes to hold collections of toys and keep them orderly. Rolling boxes are ideal for use between the lowest shelf and the floor.

▶**This whimsical chest of** drawers has storage for all childhood needs—drawers and closed cupboards for toddler clothes, open shelves for toys, and rolling bins that make a game of cleaning up kiddy clutter.

◄This child's bedchamber is a little world unto itself, with a storage ledge for prized possessions, and a spare bed stored beneath for sleepovers.

▲In addition to providing a spare bed, this bottom bunk has two large drawers for auxiliary storage.

◄A room for a school-age girl incorporates a window seat, which has drawers underneath for toys and games. Clothes are stored in the adjacent closet, where short rods and lots of pegs provide easy access to hanging items. A trunk at the foot of the bed holds off-season folded clothes. Desk drawers corral art and school supplies.

The floor is all a little kid needs for playing, but a kid-sized desk seems more grown-up and will help keep crayons and play clay off the carpet. Use storage furniture—chests of drawers, bunk beds, and shelving—for dividing a bedroom into cozy spots for various activities. Be very sure that tall furniture is secure and can't be pulled over by climbing kids. Closets should be made kid-friendly by keeping everyday

▲It's hard to get kids to hang up clothes, but keeping at least one clothes rod low will make that task a little easier. This wire shelving unit handles hanging clothes and provides shelves for folded clothes and shoes. Unlike adult closets, kid closets benefit from room on the floor to store toys and shoes.

▲This closet-top loft provides a getaway space for a 10-year-old girl, along with an enviable closet. Like a miniature playroom, complete with a beaded curtain and a double-hung window, the closet keeps all clothes in view and easy to retrieve.

clothes within reach. Look for storage solutions that require the least amount of effort: pegs instead of hangers for robes, pants, and sweatshirts; sturdy plastic hangers instead of wire hangers; open shelves instead of shelves behind doors; drawers for small, loose items, such as underwear and socks. Chests of drawers look good in a room, but they work best for babies and teens. School-age kids approach drawers like a lazy gardener tills soil—the top 4 in. of clothes are worn and replaced, while the bottom stash (perfectly clean and possibly still in style) lay dormant below. Instead, consider fitting a wall closet with shallow wire or plastic drawers and pullout shelves that allow clothes to be seen and worn—and sometimes even put away.

14

Bathroom Storage

▶**This bathroom makes use** of nooks and ledges, as well as a large medicine cabinet for the bulk of its toiletry storage.

A ah, the bathroom. Finally, you think, here's a room with simple storage needs. All a bathroom really requires is storage for towels and a few toiletries, right? Not anymore. The bathroom has voyaged light years beyond its outhouse days, when storage consisted of a nail for a flyswatter, and leagues beyond its 1950s days, when the whole family used the same bar of soap and bottle of shampoo. Today's bathrooms require storage that is more diverse and specialized than baths of yore. For instance, today's master bathroom may contain a toilet, bidet, steam shower, whirlpool tub, two sinks, and a lounging area, all of which require storage systems.

Even standard bathrooms have storage needs beyond the towel-and-toiletry basics, in large part because toiletries aren't so basic anymore. A family of any size will need a storage spot for each member's favorite shampoo, soap, and scrubbing device, not to mention each person's personal grooming paraphernalia.

Like its kitchen sister, the bathroom's myriad storage needs are best met with a wide range of storage options, from vanities to shelves to hooks and bars. As with the kitchen, the trick to effectively using limited space is figuring out what can be stored elsewhere—even if it's down the hall—and what must be kept close at hand.

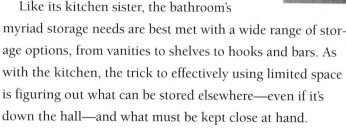

◀**This master bathroom avoids glitz and goes for elegance with a rich and charming old-**fashioned look. The lovely, dark-wood armoire protects memorabilia from the steamy environment, while storing towels and bathroom necessities. Within the cabinet, baskets further contain the clutter of toiletries.

Storage Areas to Consider

While most bathrooms are relatively small compared to other rooms in the house, they also tend to be more subdivided, with defined spaces for toilet, sink, and shower or bath. Whether or not these areas are actually partitioned off, each requires specific storage that should be customized as much as possible. When designing storage, consider the way your family uses the bathroom. For instance, take a shower with storage in mind to help you discern what's lacking: Are there too many bottles and are they constantly

▲ **This fresh and airy bathroom** keeps storage low so as not to detract from the many windows. Along with storage under the sinks, the peaceful window bench has compartments beneath the seat for backup towel storage.

◀ **This urban bathroom** contains a wealth of storage in its streamlined cabinetry. The vanity has long, shallow drawers rather than cabinets, which helps tame toiletries, while the wall cabinet provides both open and concealed storage.

◄**The bathroom vanity in this Mexican house** is a work of art that's filled with art as well. Every detail, from the beaded concrete countertop to the hammered metal sinks, adds another layer of beauty. But the art is fully functional here, providing abundant storage space for the less beautiful but still essential supplies that inhabit a bathroom.

▲**Although modest in size,** this bathroom finds the right balance between aesthetics and practical storage. The vanity cabinets provide concealed storage, while the open shelves make an attractive display of towel storage. Backup toiletries are organized in covered boxes on upper shelves.

◄**This spacious bathroom** has more storage space than most peoples' kitchens. The couple, wh ose kids have grown and moved out, even preferred storage to an extra sink, so there are drawers aplenty—17 in all—in this bank of frameless, plastic-laminate cabinetry.

Maximizing a Small Bathroom

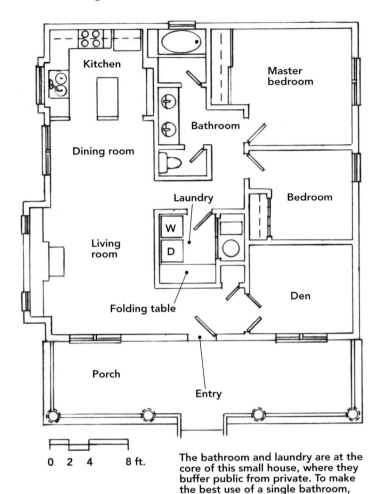

The bathroom and laundry are at the core of this small house, where they buffer public from private. To make the best use of a single bathroom, each function has its own room, and the vanity remains open and central.

Labels in floor plan: Kitchen, Master bedroom, Bathroom, Dining room, Bedroom, Laundry, W, D, Living room, Folding table, Den, Porch, Entry

Scale: 0 2 4 8 ft.

▲In a very tight house—1,048 sq. ft. for a young family of three—dividing bathroom functions makes the most sense (see the floor plan at left). The shower, vanity, and toilet each have separate but connected areas, allowing multiple occupants space and privacy. Of course, two sinks are a necessity, as are two mirrors and centralized towel storage. The washer and dryer are just across the hall from the bathroom suite.

slipping onto the shower floor? Is there a hook or bar close at hand to hang washcloths and towels? Where can you spread out a damp towel or bath mat to dry? Applying this step-by-step analysis to every part of the bathroom will help clarify your particular storage needs and how to accommodate them.

▲ **Especially in a small bathroom,** the usually dead wall space around a toilet alcove may be the perfect location for cabinetry—accessible but out of the way.

The Toilet

The toilet requires less storage than other bathroom areas, but it's very important storage—keeping extra toilet paper in the linen closet down the hall just doesn't cut it. Along with a niche for backup rolls, which could be a basket, ledge, shelf, or cabinet, it's ideal to keep toilet brush and cleanser nearby but tucked out of sight. A base cabinet would be ideal. Reading material is a traditional accompaniment, but careful placement is crucial—especially if little boys share the bathroom. A basket or magazine rack is fine as long as it's out of the way, but it does tend to collect dust and dirt. Hanging a rack on the wall near the toilet may be a better alternative, or books and magazines can be stacked on a shelf above the toilet. If your toilet is joined by a bidet, storage will be needed for soap and towels that are within easy reach.

The Sink

Consider all the activities we perform sink-side: washing, shaving, brushing, applying makeup, cleaning cuts and scrapes, soaking lingerie, and sometimes even washing hair and babies. The sink requires storage space for each of these tasks: towels, washcloths, soap, fingernail brushes, shaving gear, mouthwash, makeup, cotton balls, toothpaste, toothbrushes, first-aid supplies, and all the mentionable and unmentionable toiletries we acquire. Make it easy to store and retrieve these bathroom essentials, whether in closed cupboards, open shelves, or in a mix of deep and shallow drawers. A traditional sink vanity can handle a good portion of bathroom storage, but it can become a hindrance rather than a help if too much stuff gets tossed together randomly. Baskets, boxes, and caddies can help keep items contained within vanity closets and drawers. If you can't resist the

▲▲ **A space-saving (and visually interesting)** solution in this narrow bathroom was to keep the vanity shallow and allow the sink to extend past its boundary. Cubbies beneath keep extra beach towels within reach of the pool. The tile floor makes for quick cleanup.

▲ **This bathroom may have the standard tub-toilet-sink layout,** but its sink is quite out of the ordinary. It's supported by a cylindrical pedestal that sprouts several tiers of shelves.

▲ **A pedestal sink can be the perfect** streamlined appliance for a small bathroom, but it doesn't offer storage space. The elegant solution here is two small, freestanding cabinets built from Douglas fir.

▲Bleached-cherry V-groove beadboard creates a handsome, hardworking surface for a bathroom located near the family pool; the half-height wall with slots for reading material provides a little extra privacy and the perfect excuse to escape for a few minutes of uninterrupted reading.

▲In this master bathroom, beaded hemlock wainscoting provides an easy-to-maintain, traditional look. The half walls of wainscot define various stations in the bathroom, creating a sense of privacy while also providing natural shelving. Hooks and bars are scattered throughout for towels and robes.

beautiful lines of a pedestal sink, just keep in mind how much storage a vanity handles and make sure you have enough auxiliary storage—in the form of freestanding furniture and shelves—to compensate.

The Shower and Tub

Many master bathrooms feature both a shower and a tub. Each requires a nearby shelf, hook, or bar for a towel and washcloth or loofah; even if you opt for a shelf or hook, you'll need a bar to hang damp items, including the bath mat. A hook for a bathrobe is a nice addition, as is a place to hang clothes—either those you remove or those you'll be putting on (that steamy atmosphere can help smooth wrinkles on clothes, if not on your face). Each bathing space should contain a hamper, preferably a well-ventilated one, as well. If you have the space, you could even include more than one to sort laundry at the source.

Finding Space for Bathrooms in an Old House

Storage space is always hard to come by naturally in a 19th-century house, but finding bathroom storage can be impossible because back then, there was no such thing as an indoor bathroom. This house, first built as a one-room cottage in 1820, grew slowly over the years (in the late 1800s, one room was used as a ticket office for the commuter railroad, which still runs behind the house), but not enough to have a decent working bathroom.

Eventually, space was carved out to make a bathroom upstairs, but by the late 1980s, when architects Rick and Liz O'Leary purchased the house, it needed a serious remodel. After reframing the bathroom, Rick and Liz installed a standard 5-ft. bathtub (that's where their preschool boys are given baths). The 18-in. space left over was dedicated to a built-in column of narrow but deep shelves, which are used for towel storage (two stacks deep) and backup toiletries.

▲ **Thick wainscoting not only makes room for plumbing** but its wide cap creates a handy ledge for toiletries, too.

Just outside the bathroom on the stair landing, a hybrid cupboard stores linens for bath, bed, and table. Starting with a flea-market chest of drawers, Rick added pine sides, stiles, rails, and shelves and painted the whole assembly.

The only way to fit a bathroom downstairs was to square off an inside corner of the house. The new wall was built up and finished off with wainscoting to conceal plumbing, which also created a thick ledge that's well suited for toiletry storage. No space goes unused in this bathroom; it somehow manages to fit a 3-ft.-sq. shower flanked by a stacked washer/dryer unit. The space above is maximized by a deep shelf for towels.

▲ **There's just enough room in the bathroom** for a stacked washer/dryer unit—the shelf above offers extra linen storage. A shower curtain in front plays off the bathroom theme while hiding the unit when not in use.

▲ **This freestanding, hybrid cupboard is located just outside the bathroom** on the stair landing, providing handy storage for towels, sheets, and even tablecloths. The drawers could be used for extra or seldom-used toiletries and grooming appliances.

◀**This master bath in a city apartment has** lovely tall ceilings but not a lot of floor area. Rather than filling the limited space with a vanity, the homeowners opted for a sink with open shelves below, creating convenient and streamlined towel storage that is easily accessed from the tub. Where the toiletries are stashed is anyone's guess.

▲**This unique tub alcove keeps** bathing apparatus at hand. A towel rack and basket keep linens and robes right where they're needed, while the window ledge makes room for bath oils and soaps. The adjacent closet offers more abundant and private storage.

A well-designed shower or tub will include plenty of flat surfaces within for storing shampoo, bath oils, soap, and other bath needs. If you're building or remodeling, consider a generous tub surrounded with thick ledges or multiple niches built into the tile; otherwise, there's a variety of caddies available that either hook over the showerhead or hang in the corner. Caddies, particularly wire models, offer the advantage of easy draining and drying, which will help foil mold. Pocketed shower curtains look snappy and seem handy, but they can be prone to mildew. If space in the shower is tight or it's shared by a large family, portable caddies, which can be stored under the sink or in a closet, may be a good alternative to permanent shower storage.

Storing Toiletries and Medicine

oiletries can be loosely defined as all those bottles, tubes, and tools that we use to keep ourselves clean and looking good. Like cereals and flavors of yogurt, everyone has favorites. A family of four may very well use four—or more—different types of shampoo, while a teenager with rampant hormones requires a different kind of face cleanser than his dry-skinned mom.

Like the kitchen, the bathroom may have far more paraphernalia than it has storage space, in which case, off-site storage may need to be employed. Toiletries that are used

▲**A matching oak medicine cabinet has both** concealed and open space, allowing everyday items to be easily accessed and less frequently used (or more personal) items to be stored inside and out of the way.

▶**To reinforce the Arts and Crafts style** of their 1919 house, these homeowners replaced a style-less, built-in vanity with this pedestal sink and Craftsman-style cabinet built from quartersawn oak. Its drawers contain toiletries, while the shelves below make a convenient linen closet.

◀▼**A little chest of drawers was given new** life as a vanity by removing the drawer boxes to make room for the sink bowl and plumbing. The top drawer fronts were reattached with a bottom hinge; two small trays were installed on the panel to hold toothbrushes. The lower two drawer fronts became a cabinet drawer that conceals linens and a caddy of toiletries.

daily should be kept in the bathroom, but the bathroom equivalent of pantry storage can be devised for backup items and less frequently used toiletries, such as masques or hair coloring. The linen closet has been a traditional warehouse for toiletry storage, but items tend to get lost on its deep shelves; consider installing a vertical column of narrow shelves on one wall of the closet, which will help keep order. If you're building or remodeling, look at pantry design for inspiration and consider including a shallow closet specifically dedicated to toiletry storage.

The Vanity

The traditional, built-in vanity is slightly shorter (32 in. as opposed to 36 in.) and often more shallow than the standard 2-ft.-deep kitchen cabinet. Like the kitchen cabinet, however, vanity cabinet cases and doors are most often built from plywood or medium-density fiberboard (MDF) that's been given a wood-veneer, plastic-laminate, or melamine finish.

▼**This cheerful bathroom belongs to an artist** who has added spark to this straightforward bathroom with fanciful touches such as the tiled floor and bold sink fixtures. Even the standard (but highly efficient), off-the-shelf vanity has been given an artsy, modern flare with circular finger pulls in place of traditional hardware.

▲**This 21-in.-deep vanity has** space-saving sliding doors, which make an aesthetic statement, while keeping this very narrow bathroom maneuverable.

Some face-frames are built from solid wood. And bathroom cabinets are no less blessed than their kitchen cousins with any number of stock or custom-designed inserts and configurations that will help you corral toiletries. A vanity doesn't have to be built-in, however. A freestanding table, chest, or waist-high shelf unit can stand in for the traditional vanity cabinet, even to the extent of containing the sink and its plumbing.

A vanity can be fitted with an assortment of drawers, doors, and even open shelving, depending on what kind of toiletries you plan to store there. Whatever configuration you chose, include substantial closed cabinetry—drawers and doors—which is essential in a bathroom. Shallow drawers work best for makeup and smaller grooming products, but partitions, boxes, baskets, or caddies can help tame

◄**A chunky, English-style table makes a big**
statement as a vanity, with two sink bowls set
into the marble countertop. The apron is so
deep that it hides the sink bowls and most of
the plumbing from view, while still providing
room for storage and display. A medicine cabinet with substantial crown molding balances the
table's heft and provides lots of storage.

small toiletries in a larger drawer. Drawers that will be used
for active toiletry storage should be positioned just to the
side of a sink or between two sinks for easiest accessibility.

Shelves are also useful in a vanity. Pullout shelves are almost as easy to access as drawers and make a good supple-
ment to drawer storage for toiletries that are used daily.
Fixed shelving works well for backup or infrequently used
toiletries. Open shelves and ledges can be an aesthetically
pleasing addition to vanity configurations and are perfect for
toiletries that are pretty and colorful (as well as handy to
have right at hand), such as perfume, makeup brushes, or
decorative jars that hold cotton swabs or cotton balls.

▲**This vanity ingeniously unites the master**
bedroom and bath suite, bridging the gap between the wood floor of the former and limestone tile of the latter. The unique design of its
drawers and cabinets further defines space and
function: Once they hit the limestone, they jut
out from the section of vanity that resides on
the bedroom side of the borderline. The vanity's
concrete countertop follows suit, curving out
from the wall to attach to the end of the tub.

The Medicine Cabinet

A traditional in-wall medicine cabinet is not a necessity if there's sufficient storage in vanity drawers, on linen closet shelves, or in countertop caddies. But there's something to be said for the naturally restricted space of a recessed medicine cabinet, with its shallow, removable, easy-to-keep-clean glass shelves, and its high placement—usually a deterrent to small children. Yet medicine cabinets aren't always the best bet for storing medicines. The bathroom is not the cool, dry place that most medicines require for storage, and many medicine cabinets aren't lockable.

The medicine cabinet is ideal for small toiletries that you use every day—a razor, nail scissors, cotton balls, alcohol, and basic cosmetics. Provide narrow, open containers, such as a soap dish, to collect the stuff that tends to roll or tip out. Or copy the design in your refrigerator door and provide a little lip or railing on the edge of the shelves. Don't

▼**A bathroom under the eaves** is a cozy and bright space with the addition of a skylight. A small medicine cabinet and a single glass shelf provide storage for bathroom basics, which is all that is needed in this secondary half-bath.

▲**In this master bathroom,** drawers and cabinets provide a good mix of storage, while a medicine cabinet (behind the side mirror) makes everyday items easy to reach.

◄A recessed medicine cabinet is just one of the details that helps this new house look old. The pedestal sink is an authentic addition, but it's behind the times in terms of storage. However, the medicine cabinet and wainscoting niches provide enough room for everyday toiletries.

▲The new master bathroom in this old house shows off a rustic medicine cabinet built from salvaged barn lumber, complete with an old barn window.

store occasionally used toiletries here; relegate them to a linen closet or vanity along with back-stock toiletries. While mirrors make natural doors for medicine cabinets that hang over a sink, there's no reason you can't put a medicine cabinet to one side and give it a glazed or solid door.

Childproof Storage

In families with small children, it's essential that any medicines, prescription or over-the-counter, are stored up high in lockable cabinets or closets. And it's not just medicine that's potentially dangerous to young children. Many adult toiletries, most first-aid treatments, and certainly cleaning materials are potentially toxic. It's so much easier to keep a bathroom clean if cleaning materials are kept there as well, but it's more important to keep them out of reach of small children. Install truly childproof locks (not the easily breached plastic clips that fit on the inside) on cabinets that contain dangerous materials.

Storing Bathroom Linens

The linen closet doesn't have to be a 2-ft.-by-2-ft. alcove with a door. A tall built-in cabinet, a freestanding hutch or armoire, or open-shelf units are all good storage alternatives for towels, washcloths, and toilet paper. Regardless of where you store them, towels should be rotated to prevent uneven fading.

►**This lovely but modest-sized** bathroom provides simple but varied storage for towels—on a stainless-steel rod under the sink, in a basket under the vanity, and in built-in cubbies trimmed with a beaded edge. While the latter provides back-up storage, this quaint basket can be pulled over to the bathtub, allowing the bather to pull a fresh towel without dripping all over the floor.

Storage That Moves: Carts and Caddies

Portable containers for toiletries and towels make a lot of sense in a bathroom, particularly when it has multiple users and limited space. Divvy up toiletries by family member so that everyone has the day's toiletries at hand in one basket, which can be carted from closet to sink to shower. Or sort toiletries by type and designate a shower-bound caddy and a sink-side one.

A rolling cart can be a very efficient storage option as well. Like caddies, a cart will allow you to stash paraphernalia out of the way while still keeping it accessible. But with a cart, the entire spectrum of your grooming needs—towels, toiletries, and even appliances—can be kept in one convenient place.

▲Plastic caddies hold everyday toiletries in this small bathroom, making them a breeze to cart to sink or tub and then put back in the linen closet when grooming is done.

▲This lovely urban bathroom has lighter-than-air storage in the form of a delicate rack for towels and toiletries. Keeping storage light helps make the space feel bigger.

▲The windowsill in this Martha's Vineyard house was widened and fitted with a 2-in.-wide slot, which functions as a towel rack. Hooks in the wainscoting trim are handy for additional towels, robes, and clothing.

▲This pine linen cabinet was inspired by the simplicity of early American furniture. It provided enough room for towels and toiletries so that the homeowners could sacrifice a vanity for a traditional pedestal sink.

Have you ever been in a bathroom with too many towel bars and hooks? Probably not. It never hurts to install more towel bars than you think you'll need, although finding the space for them may be tough. Be inventive: Recess the front of a vanity and install a wide towel bar just below the countertop. And don't ignore the back of the door: Two towel bars can fit here, as can a peg rail with hooks for towels or bathrobes.

Resources

PROFESSIONAL ORGANIZATIONS

American Institute of Architects (AIA)

1735 New York Avenue NW
Washington, DC 20006
www.aia.org
Lists architects who are members of AIA. The website allows you to search for AIA architects in your area.

American Society of Interior Designers (ASID)

608 Massachusetts Avenue NE
Washington, DC 20002
www.asid.org For names of ASID members
in your area, go to the referral website: www.interiors.org

National Association of Professional Organizers (NAPO)

4700 West Lake Avenue
Glenview, IL 60025
www.napo.net
Lists professional organizers who are members of NAPO. Go to the referral section of the site to find a professional organizer in your area.

National Association of the Remodeling Industry (NARI®)

4900 Seminary Road, #3210
Alexandria, VA 22311
(800) 6111-6274
www.nari.org

National Kitchen and Bath Association

687 Willow Grove Street
Hackettstown, NJ 07840
www.nkba.com
Members are kitchen and bath design specialists. The website has projects, remodeling tips, and lists design guidelines.

CONTAINERS AND ORGANIZING SUPPLIES

Bed Bath & Beyond®
(800) 462-3966
www.bedbathandbeyond.com
A wide range of affordable storage and organizing solutions for all areas of the home.

Broadway Panhandler
477 Broome Street
New York, NY 10013
(866) 266-5927
www.broadwaypanhandler.com
Specialty cookware, kitchen supplies, and storage solutions.

Casabella®
(800) 841-4140
www.casabella.com

CD Storehouse
(800) 829-4203
CD storage solutions.

The Container Store®
(888) 266-8246
www.containerstore.com
Closet systems, storage containers, and useful organizing tools.

Exposures®
(800) 222-4947
www.exposuresonline.com
Photo storage materials.

Filofax®
www.filofax.com
Calendars and daily planners.

Freedom Bag®
(877) 573-3366
www.freedombag.com
Makeup, jewelry, and other travel bags.

Frontgate®
(800) 626-6488
www.frontgate.com
Innovative storage solutions for garages, basements, kitchens and other hard-working areas of the home.

Hold Everything®
(800) 421-2264
www.holdeverything.com
Kitchen, bed, bath, and home-office organizing gear.

Levenger®
(800) 544-0880
www.levenger.com
Home office supplies.

Rubbermaid
(888) 895-2110
www.rubbermaid.com
Containers for closets, garages, and basements.

Stacks and Stacks
(800) 761-5222
www.stacksandstacks.com
Shelving and storage solutions.

Tupperware
(800) 366-3800
www.tupperware.com
Food storage.

Umbra
(800) 327-5122
www.umbra.com
Office and bathroom storage.

FURNISHINGS

The Conran Shop
407 East 59th Street
New York, NY 10022
(212) 755-9079
www.conran.com
Functional, modern furnishings for every room of the house.

Crate & Barrel
(800) 996-9960
www.crateandbarrel.com
Wide range of contemporary and modern furnishings for all rooms.

Design Within Reach
(800) 944-2233
www.dwr.com
Cutting-edge furnishings with a functional focus.

Gracious Home
1992 Broadway
New York, NY 10022
(212) 231-7800
www.gracioushome.com
A wide range of decorative and practical storage solutions and other furnishings.

Ikea®
www.ikea.com
Contemporary furnishings and DIY storage solutions for every room of the house.

Kmart™
(866) 562-7848
www.kmart.com
Cleaning supplies and storage solutions for all areas of the home.

Restoration Hardware
www.restorationhardware.com
Vintage-style storage solutions for kitchens, baths, and other hardworking spaces.

Target®
(800) 800-8800
www.target.com
Cleaning supplies and storage solutions for kitchens, baths, basements, and garages.

STORAGE SYSTEMS

California Closets®
www.californiaclosets.com
Customized storage solutions for areas of the home.

Closet Factory
(310) 715-1000
www.closetfactory.com
Custom closet solutions.

ClosetMaid®
(800) 874-0008
www.closetmaid.com
Storage solutions for every room of the house.

Poliform
(888) 765-4367
www.poliformusa.com
Modern closet solutions.

Rubbermaid
(888) 895-2110
www.rubbermaid.com
DIY closet solutions.

KITCHEN CABINETS

Bulthaup
www.bulthaup.com
Modern kitchen systems.

Knape & Vogt
(616) 459-3311
www.knapeandvogt.com
Organizing accessories for kitchen cabinets.

Kraftmaid
(800) 571-1990
www.kraftmaid.com
Kitchen cabinets stocked with smart organizing solutions.

Rev-A-Shelf®
(800) 626-1126
www.rev-a-shelf.com
Solutions for maximizing cabinet shelf space.

PUBLICATIONS

Mendelson, Cheryl. *Home Comforts: The Art and Science of Keeping House*. New York: Scribner, 1999.

Home Comforts is a great source of the minutiae of housekeeping, but you can take what you like when you need it, thanks to a detailed index. The entire book is filled with ideas either directly or obliquely related to household storage, such as maintaining a pantry and folding clothes. I still like my own way of folding socks and I just can't follow her schedule for cleaning out a refrigerator, but I'm willing to take Mendelson's advice on many things, such as caring for books, storing linens, and the value of keeping a reasonably organized house.

Morse, Edward W. *Japanese Homes and Their Surroundings*. New York: Dover Publications, 1961.

Dover, bless its heart, reprinted this 1886 book, written by a scientist who visited Japan to study brachiopods and became enamored of the Japanese house. Morse wrote clearly and with great admiration for traditional Japanese design, before it was much influenced by the West. His illustrations are precise and charming. The book presents quite a few storage ideas, from towel racks to tansu chests, along with relaying an underlying concept of function inseparable from beauty.

Norman, Donald. *The Design of Everyday Things*. New York: Doubleday, 1990.

This reissued book is aimed at students and aficionados of product design. It is slightly behind the times in terms of the latest products, but it is timeless in its critique of product design, and a fun read. Norman says that there are perhaps 20,000 everyday things, including bulbs, sockets, clocks, paper clips, and scissors. Each object is made of several, if not many parts: a desk stapler has 16 parts, and so on. Norman may not analyze specific home storage products—he critiques car hardware, for example—but his logic applies to the things we use at home.

Ordesky, Maxine. *The Complete Home Organizer*. New York: Grove Press, 1993.

Ordesky is obsessed with organization and dreams about closet space, and it shows in this book, subtitled "A Guide to Functional Storage Space for All the Rooms in Your Home." She presents many ideas for efficient storage, with a focus on the various details of organizing space for clothes.

Martha Stewart Living Omnimedia, Inc. *Good Things with Martha Stewart Living: Good Things for Organizing*. New York: Clarkson Potter/Publishers, 2001.

This paperback book is worth a look-see for clever storage ideas that can spruce up each room, including make-it-yourself elements that the magazine is known for, such as a ribboned message board and a window shelf.

Rybczynski, Witold. *Home: A Short History of an Idea*. New York: Viking Penguin, 1986.

I reread this book every now and then because, like E. B. White's essays, it's so readable and thoughtful. This isn't a how-to book at all, but a book that dwells on the physical elements that make the house a comfortable place.

Calloway, Stephen, and Elizabeth Cromley (Eds.). *The Elements of Style*. New York: Simon & Schuster, 1996.

This fat book is an excellent visual reference for designers and homeowners who deal with period houses (this book covers from 1485 to the present). Color-coded tabs call out the various elements of a house, from services (bathrooms) to built-ins. It's an expensive book, but there's a lot of information here, packed into a lot of drawings and photos of English (and a few other European examples) and American period homes, many historically significant.

Jackson, Shirley. *Raising Demons*. New York: Popular Library, 1979.

I just had to add this because of its first chapter. This memoir of chaotic family life (in the 1950s) is out of print, but it's likely to be in your library. Shirley starts the book by describing the hundredth day of trying to close the door on a closet jam-packed with sports gear. This initiates a many-month hunt for a bigger house for her family of six. After house-hunting, scraping up the down payment, and packing hundreds of boxes, the family moves. Shirley finally unpacks the last hockey stick and puts it in the hall closet—and the door won't close.

Taunton Press Publications

The *Fine Homebuilding* division of The Taunton Press has published a number of books with many storage ideas, including my own *The Kitchen Idea Book, The Bathroom Idea Book* by Andrew Wormer, *The Kidspace Idea Book* by Wendy A. Jordan, and *At Work at Home* by Neal Zimmerman. Also check out *Fine Homebuilding* magazine and its special annual issues, Houses and Kitchens and Baths.

Fine Woodworking magazine is a great resource for ideas and techniques for making various storage devices, such as book-

cases, cabinets, and toolboxes. I referred to *Fine Woodworking* for a detailed discussion and drawings of secret compartments in furniture and cabinetry. Look for Chris Becksvoort's fascinating article, "Secret Compartments," in *Fine Woodworking* #74, Jan./Feb. 1989, pp. 42-46. Many *Fine Woodworking* books focus on storage furniture. Take a look at *Built-In Furniture* by Jim Tolpin, *The Shaker Legacy* by Christian Becksvoort, *Treasure Chests* by Lon Schleining, and *Bookcases* by Niall Barrett.

Web Sites

The Web has evolved far beyond the primordial soup it was just a few years ago, but consistent quality and ease of navigation are still elusive. Type "home storage" into a search engine and you'll get three million hits. Exclude any links to storing data and the list shrinks by one-half. So

how do you find the good stuff? One trick is to be as specific as possible. Search for "tie racks," "closet systems," or "silverware drawer inserts" to get better results. Another approach is to take advantage of other people's research by visiting the Web sites of home design magazines, information companies, and associations. Many have compiled links to the sites they like, whether for products or information. Here are a few sites that present information about storage design and product, as well as links to other sites that you might find useful:

www.period-homes.com

This Web site is run by Period Homes Magazine, one of Clem Labine's resourceful publications (Labine's Traditional Building focuses on commercial and civic projects, but it's relevant to houses, too). They call it "Your Internet Portal to Suppliers of

Historically Styled Residential Products," and that's what it is, a link to the actual Web sites of manufacturers who make products for pre-1940 houses and new homes built in traditional styles. Look for mantels, wine racks, cabinets, and chests among the many storage products.

www.build.com

This is called "The Building and Home Improvement Directory" and it's been around since 1994, which makes it ancient for a Web company. You'll find links to manufacturers of building products, online merchants of home products, building publications, and a big list of builders, designers, real estate agents, and mortgage brokers.

www.access-board.gov/
A federal agency committed to accessible design sponsors this

Web site, which offers news and technical bulletins on design and provides downloadable guidelines of the Americans with Disabilities Act (ADA).

www.taunton.com/fhb
The Web site of *Fine Homebuilding* magazine contains links to an ever-growing list of manufacturers, publications about building, and information sites. Categories include Kit Homes, Environmentally Conscious Building, Hardware, Kitchen and Bath, and an incredibly long section on tools. There are also links to information sources, such as oikos.com, a "green" building source, which in turn provides links to energy-efficient publications, news, and products.

The information on Fine Homebuilding's own site can be a good source of products and design ideas as well, with virtual tours of houses and a sampling of articles from the magazine, plus Web-only content. This is also where you can access Breaktime, an active—and I do mean active—forum for people interested in home design. It's an excellent source for opinions about storage, among other things, such as how to build bookshelf supports and how to lay out a kitchen. Take a look at www.taunton.com/fc for Fine Cooking's informative Web site and its forum, Cook's Talk, which is another source of ideas for kitchen design. I've picked up some great tips on kitchen storage (and life) from the generous and passionate regulars on this forum.

Credits

p. 6: Photo © davidduncanlivingston.com.

p. 7: Photo: Scott Gibson © The Taunton Press, Inc.; cabinetmaker: Serge Therrien, Sonoma, CA.

CHAPTER 1

p. 8: Photo © Eric Roth

p. 10: (bottom) Photo courtesy of The Schulte Corporation; (top) Photo © Eric Roth

p. 11: Photo © Eric Roth

p. 12: Photo by Andy Engel, © The Taunton Press, Inc.

p. 13: (left) Photo by Scott Gibson, © The Taunton Press, Inc.; (top right) Photo by Greg Premru, © The Taunton Press, Inc.

p. 14: Photos © Eric Piasecki

p. 15: Photo by Scott Gibson,

© The Taunton Press, Inc.

p 16: Photo © Joshua McHugh; Design by Eileen Kasofsky

p. 17: (top) Photo © Eric Roth; (bottom) Photo © Wendell T. Webber.

CHAPTER 2

p. 18: Photo © Brian Vanden Brink

p 20: (left) Photo © 2005 www.carolynbates.com; (right) Photo © Melabee M. Miller

p. 21: (left) Photo © Wendell T. Webber; (right) Photo © Phillip Ennis; Design by Ronald Bricke

p. 23: (top) Photo © Rob Karosis/www.robkarosis.com; (bottom left) Photo © 2005 www.carolynbates.com; (bottom right) Photo © Robert Perron, photographer

p. 24: (top left & right) Photos © Brian Vanden Brink; (bottom left) Photo © Chipper Hatter

p. 25: (top) Photo © Brian Vanden Brink; (bottom) Photo © Wendell T. Webber

p. 26: (top) Photo © Wendell T. Webber; (bottom) Photo by Karen Tanaka, © The Taunton Press, Inc.

p. 27: (top left) Photo © Phillip Ennis; Design by Joyce Dixon; (top right) Photo by Charles Miller, © The Taunton Press, Inc.; (bottom) Photo © Brian Vanden Brink.

p. 28: Photo © Brian Vanden Brink

p. 30: (top) Photo © Eric Piasecki; (bottom) Photo © Tim Street-Porter

p. 31: (left) Photo © Brian Vanden Brink; (right) Photo © Melabee M. Miller

p. 32: (left) Photo © Tim Street-Porter; (top right) Photo © 2005 www.carolynbates.com; (bottom right) Photo © Mark Samu

p. 33: Photo © Susan Kahn

p.34: (left) Photo © Robert Perron; (right) Photo © 2005 www.carolynbates.com

p. 35: (bottom) Photo by Roe A. Osborn, © The Taunton Press, Inc.; (top left) Photo © 2005 www.carolynbates.com; (top right) Photo © Phillip Ennis; Design by DNA/Dineen Nealy Architects

p. 36: (top left) Photo © Wendell T. Webber; (bottom left) Photo © Brian Vanden Brink; (right) Photo © Melabee M. Miller

p. 37: (top) Photo © Mark Samu; (bottom) Photo © 2005 www.carolynbates.com

p. 38: (left) Photo by Karen Tanaka, © The Taunton Press, Inc.; (top right) Photo by Charles Miller, © The Taunton Press, Inc.; (bottom right) Photo © Robert Perron

p. 39: Photo © Melabee M. Miller

p. 40: (top left) Photo © Robert Perron, photographer; (top right) Photo © Tim Street-Porter; (bottom left) Photo © Eric Piasecki

p. 41: (top) Photo © 2005 www.carolynbates.com; (bottom) Photo © Brian Vanden Brink

p. 42: (left & bottom right) Photos © Brian Vanden Brink; (top right) Photo © Mark Samu

p. 43: (top) Photo © John Gruen; (bottom) Photo © Phillip Ennis; Design by Mojo Stumer, Architects

p. 44: Photo © Tim Street-Porter

p. 45: (left) Photo © Tim Street-Porter; (top right) Photo by Chris Green, © The Taunton Press, Inc.; (bottom right) Photo © Phillip Ennis; Design by JFMP/Jones, Footer, Margeotes Partners, Inc.

p. 46: Photo © Brian Vanden Brink

p. 47: (left) Photo © 2005 www.carolynbates.com; (top right) Photo © Phillip Ennis; Design by Ronald Bricke; (bottom right) Photo © Brian Vanden Brink

p. 48: (left) Photo © Melabee M. Miller; (top) Photo © Rob Karosis/www.robkarosis.com; (center) Photo © Tim Street-Porter; (bottom) Photo © Brian Vanden Brink

p. 49: Photo © Brian Vanden Brink

p. 50: (top left) Photo © Eric Piasecki; (center & right) Photo © Melabee M. Miller; (bottom left) Photo by Roe A. Osborn, © The Taunton Press, Inc.

p. 51: (left) Photo © Mark Samu; (right) Photo © Melabee M. Miller.

CHAPTER 4

p. 52: Photo © Eric Piasecki

p. 54: (top) Photo © Chipper Hatter; (bottom) Photo © Robert Perron, photographer

p. 55: (left) Photo © Tim Street-Porter; (right) Photo © Phillip Ennis; Design by K Design/Fred Kentop

p. 56: Photo © Eric Piasecki

p. 57: (top and bottom left)Photo © Melabee M. Miller; (right: top, center & bottom) Photos © Wendell T. Webber

p. 58: (top left) Photo © Povy Kendal Atchison; (bottom left) Photo © Roger Turk/Northlight Photography, Inc.; (right) Photo © Eric Roth

p. 59: Photo © Eric Roth

p. 60: Photo © Tim Street-Porter

p. 61: (left) Photo © Rob Karosis/www.robkarosis.com; (top right) Photo © Eric Roth; (bottom right) Photo © 2005 www.carolynbates.com

p. 62: (top) Photo © Sandy Agrafiotis, photographer; (bottom) Photo © Eric Piasecki

p. 63: (top) Photo © Norman McGrath; (bottom) Photo © Brian Vanden Brink

p. 64: (left) Photo © davidduncanlivingston.com; (right, top & bottom) Photos © Brian Vanden Brink

p. 65: Photo © Eric Roth.

p. 66: Photo © Tim Street-Porter

p. 68: (left) Photo © Tim Street-Porter; (right) Photo © Brian Vanden Brink

p. 69: Photos © Brian Vanden Brink

p. 70: Photo © Rob Karosis/www.robkarosis.com

p. 71: (left, top & bottom) Photos © Tim Street-Porter; (right) Photo © www.stevevierraphotography.com

p. 72: (left) Photo © Brian Vanden Brink; (right) Photo © Wendell T. Webber

p. 73: Photo © Phillip Ennis; Design by Interior Consultants/Denise Balassi

p. 74: (top) Photo © Mark Samu; (bottom) Photo © Tim Street-Porter

p. 75: (left) Photo © Eric Roth; (right) Photo © Wendell T. Webber

p. 76: (top) Photo © Mark Samu

p. 77: (left) Photo © Wendell T. Webber; (top right) Photo © Melabee M. Miller; (bottom right) Photo © Wendell T. Webber

p. 78: (top left) Photo © Susan Kahn; (bottom left) Photo © Phillip Ennis; Design by KAT Interiors; (right) Photo © Phillip Ennis; Design by BT Designs

p. 79: (left) Photo © Phillip Ennis; Design by Bradley, Klein, Thiergartner; (right) Photo by Phillip Ennis; Design by BT Designs

p. 80: (bottom left) Photo © 2005 www.carolynbates.com; (top left & right) Photos © Brian Vanden Brink; (right) Photo © Mark Samu

p. 81: (top) Photo © Phillip Ennis; (bottom) Photo © Brian Vanden Brink

p. 82: (top left) Photo © Brian Vanden Brink; (bottom left) Photo © Mark Samu; (right) Photo © Jessie Walker

p. 83: Photo © Phillip Ennis; Design by Bradley, Klein, Thiergartner.

CHAPTER 6

p. 84: Photo © Alise O'Brien

p. 86: (bottom left) Photo © Phillip Ennis; Design by Fergusen, Shamamian & Ratner; (top right) Photo © Melabee M. Miller

p. 87: (top left & top right) Photos © Wendell T. Webber; (bottom) Photo courtesy California Closet Co., Inc.

p. 88: (left) Photo © Melabee M. Miller; (bottom right) Photo courtesy Georgia-Pacific Corporation; (top right) Photo © Wendell T. Webber

p. 89: (bottom) Photo © Melabee M. Miller; (top) Photo © Michael Mathers

p. 90: (left) Photo © Brian Vanden Brink; (right) Photo © Tim Street-Porter

p. 91: (top) Photo © John Umberger; (bottom) Photo courtesy California Closet Co., Inc.

p. 92: (top) Photo courtesy The Land of Nod; (bottom) Photo © Joshua McHugh; Design by Eileen Kasofsky

p. 93: Photo © Olson Photographic, LLC

p. 94: (left) Photo © Tim Street-Porter; (top right) Photo © Kathy Detwiler Lee; (bottom right) Photo © Wendell T. Webber

p. 95 Photos © Wendell T. Webber

p. 96: Photo © Phillip Ennis; Design by Fergusen, Shamamian & Ratner

p. 97: (right) Photo courtesy SmithandVansant.com; (left, top to bottom) Photos © Wendell T. Webber

p. 98: (left) Photo © Joshua McHugh, styling by Eileen Kasofsky; (right) Photo courtesy The Land of Nod

p. 99: (right) Photo © Wendell T. Webber; (left) Photo courtesy The Land of Nod

p. 100: (right) Photo © Wendell T. Webber; (left) Photo © Chipper Hatter

p. 101: (left & bottom right) Photos © Wendell T. Webber; (top right) Photo courtesy Pottery Barn

p. 102: Photos © Wendell T. Webber

p. 103: (left) Photo © Joshua McHugh; Design by Eileen Kasofsky; (right, top & bottom) Photos © Wendell T. Webber.

CHAPTER 7

p. 104: Photo © Wendell T. Webber

p. 106: (top) Photo © Eric Piasecki; (bottom) Photo © Brian Vanden Brink

p. 107: (top left & bottom right) Photos © Wendell T. Webber; (right) Photo © Tim Street-Porter

p. 108: (left) Photo © Rob Karosis/www.robkarosis.com; (right) Photo © davidduncanlivingston.com

p. 109: (top left) Photo © Wendell T. Webber; (bottom left) Photo © Rob Karosis/www.robkarosis.com; (top right) Photo © Lee Anne White; (bottom right) Photo © Alise O'Brien

p. 110: (left & bottom right) Photos © davidduncanlivingston.com; (top right) Photo © Roger Turk/Northlight Photography Inc.

p. 111: Photo © Tim Street-Porter

p. 112: (top) Photo © 2005 www.carolynbates.com; (bottom) Photo © Rob Karosis/www.robkarosis.com

p. 113: Photo © Brian Vanden Brink

p. 114: Photo © Wendell T. Webber

p. 115: (left) Photo © Wendell T. Webber; (top right) Photo © Robert Perron, photographer; (bottom right) Photo © Phillip Ennis; Design by Reger Designs

p. 116: Photo © Rob Karosis/www.robkarosis.com

p. 117: (top left) Photo © Lee Anne White; (top center) Photo © Wendell T. Webber; (top right) Photo © Roger Turk/Northlight Photography Inc.; (bottom) Photo © Rob Karosis/www.robkarosis.com

p. 118: (top) Photo by John Rickard, © The Taunton Press, Inc.; (bottom) Photo © Melabee M. Miller

p. 119: (left) Photo by John Rickard, © The Taunton Press, Inc.; (right) Photo by Jerry Bates, © The Taunton Press, Inc.

p. 120: (top) Photo © Lee Anne White; (bottom) Photo courtesy Gladiator GarageWorks

p. 121: (top right) Photo by Jerry Bates, © The Taunton Press, Inc.; (center right) Photo courtesy Home Focus; (left & bottom right) Photos by John Rickard, © The Taunton Press, Inc.

CHAPTER 8

p. 122: Photo: © Durston Saylor; design: Kaehler Moore Architects.

p. 124: (left) Photo © Durston Saylor; design: Kaehler Moore Architects, Greenwich, CT; (right) photo © davidduncanlivingston.com.

p. 125: Photo: Charles Bickford © The Taunton Press, Inc.; design: Dan Rockhill, Lawrence, KS.

p. 126: Photo © David Ericson; design: Patrick W. McClane, Richmond, VA.

p. 127: (left) Photo © Joanne Bouknight; (right) photo: Charles Miller © The Taunton

Press, Inc.; design: Kurt Lavenson, Alamo. CA.

pp. 128-130: Photos © davidduncanlivingston.com; design: South Mountain Company, West Tisbury, MA.

p. 130: Photos © Charles Register; design: (left) Ellen Weinstein, Dixon Weinstein Architects, and Betsy West & Dee Blackburn, Chapel Hill, NC; (right) Dixon Weinstein Architects, Chapel Hill, NC.

p. 131: Photo © Randy O'Rourke; design: Pete di Girolamo, Salerno, Livingston Architects, San Diego, CA; ceramic design: Connie di Girolamo; cabinetry: Glen Stewart, San Diego, CA.

p. 132: (left) Photos: Charles Miller © The Taunton Press, Inc.; design: Kathryn Porter, Oakland, CA; (right) photo © Charles Register; design: Dixon Weinstein Architects, Chapel Hill, NC.

p. 133: Photo © Ken Gutmaker; design: Austin Patterson Disston Architects, Southport, CT.

p. 134: Photo © Durston Saylor; design: Kaehler Moore Architects, Greenwich, CT.

p. 135: (left) Photo © Randy O'Rourke; design: Austin Patterson Disston Architects, Southport, CT; (right) photo © Susan Kahn; design: Liz and Rick O'Leary, Croton Falls, NY.

p. 137: (top left and right) Photo © Geoffrey Gross; design: Deborah T. Lipner, Ltd., and Kaehler Moore Architects, Greenwich, CT; (bottom left and right) photo: Kevin Ireton © The Taunton Press, Inc.; design: Louis Mackall, Breakfast Woodworks, Branford, CT.

p. 138: Photo: Charles Miller © The Taunton Press, Inc.; design: Jon Stoumen.

p. 140: (left) Photo © Derrill Bazzy; design: South Mountain Company, West Tisbury, MA; (right) photo © Robert Perron; design: Banks Design Associates.

p. 141: (left) Photo: Andy Engel © The Taunton Press, Inc.; design: Daryl S. Rantis, Fayetteville, AR; (right) photo: Charles Miller © The Taunton Press, Inc.; design: Robert B. Reed, Bellevue, WA.

p. 142: Photo: Kevin Ireton © The Taunton Press, Inc.; design: Sarah Susanka, Mulfinger & Susanka Architects, Minneapolis, MN.

p. 143: (left) Photo © Charles Register; design: Dixon Weinstein Architects, Chapel Hill, NC; (right) photo © Grey Crawford; design: Barry Svigals, New Haven, CT.

p. 144: Photo: Charles Miller © The Taunton Press, Inc.; design: James Estes, Newport, RI.

p. 145: (left) Photo: Charles Miller © The Taunton Press, Inc.; design: Kurt Lavenson, Alamo, CA; (right) photo © Robert Benson; design: Austin Patterson Disston Architects, Southport, CT.

p. 146: Photos: Charles Bickford © The Taunton Press, Inc.; design: Lynn Hopkins, Lexington, MA.

p. 147: Photo: Kevin Ireton © The Taunton Press, Inc.; design: Margaret Bakker and Rob Lewis, Shavertown, PA; builder: Michael Millner, Pittsford, NY.

p. 148: (left) Photo: Charles Bickford © The Taunton Press, Inc.; design: Sulkin+Mills, Los Angeles, CA; (right): photo: Charles Miller © The Taunton Press, Inc.; design: Harry N. Pharr, Warwick, NY.

p. 149: Photo: Charles Miller © The Taunton Press, Inc.; design: Keith Moskow, Boston, MA.

p. 150: Photo © davidduncanlivingston.com.

p. 151: Photos © Robert Benson; design: Austin Patterson Disston Architects, Southport, CT.

p. 152-153: Photos © Randy O'Rourke; design: Austin Patterson Disston Architects, Southport, CT.

p. 154: Photos © Randy O'Rourke; design: Kaehler Moore Architects, Greenwich, CT.

p. 155: Photo © Geoffrey Gross; design: Deborah T. Lipner, Ltd., and Kaehler Moore Architects, both of Greenwich, CT.

p. 156: Photo: Charles Miller © The Taunton Press, Inc.; design: Mac White, Michael G. Imber, Architect, San Antonio, TX.

p. 158: Photo: Charles Miller © The Taunton Press, Inc.; design: Mark Priester, Priester's Cabinets, and Cynthia Smith, St. Augustine, FL.

p. 159: Photos © Randi Baird; design: South Mountain Company, West Tisbury, MA.

p. 160: Photo © James West; design: Dixon Weinstein Architects, Chapel Hill, NC.

p. 161: (top) Photo © davidduncanlivingston.com; (middle) photo: Charles Miller © The Taunton Press, Inc.; design: James Estes, Newport, RI; (bottom) photo: Roe A. Osborn © The Taunton Press, Inc.; design: David D. Quillin; cabinetry: dougmockett.com

pp. 162-163: Photos: Kevin Ireton © The Taunton Press, Inc.; design: Geoff Prentiss, Seattle, WA.

p. 164: Photos: Kevin Ireton © The Taunton Press, Inc.; architect: Tom Vermeland, Minneapolis, MN.

p. 165: Photo: Charles Miller © The Taunton Press, Inc.; cabinetmaker: Charles Chandler, Milwaukee, WI.

p. 166: (left) Photo: Charles Bickford © The Taunton Press, Inc.; design: Ron DiMauro; cabinetmaker: Glenn Sherman; (right) photo © davidduncanlivingston.com.

p. 167: (top) Photo: Scott Gibson © The Taunton Press, Inc.; design: Ken Wolosin, Taos, NM; (bottom) photo © davidduncanlivingston.com.

p. 168: Photos © davidduncanlivingston.com.

p. 169: (top) Photo © Robert Perron; design: L. Banks; photo © davidduncanlivingston.com.

p. 170: Photos © davidduncanlivingston.com.

p.171: (left) Photo © Robert Perron; design: Doug Williamson, Guilford, CT; (right) photo: Scott Gibson © The Taunton Press, Inc.; cabinetmaker: Rex Alexander, Brethren, MI.

pp. 172–174: Photos © davidduncanlivingston.com.

p. 175: Photo: Charles Miller © The Taunton Press, Inc.; design: House + House, San Francisco, CA.

p. 176: Photo: Charles Miller © The Taunton Press, Inc.; design: Fu-Tung Cheng, Cheng Design, Berkeley, CA.

p. 177: Photo © davidduncanlivingston.com.

p. 178-179: Photos © Susan Kahn; design: Liz and Rick O'Leary, Croton Falls, NY.

p. 180: Photos © davidduncanlivingston.com.

p. 181: (top) Photo: Scott Gibson © The Taunton Press, Inc.; design: William F. Roslansky, Woods Hold, MA; (bottom) photo © davidduncanlivingston.com.

p. 182: Photo © Tom O'Brien; architect: Holly B. Cratsley, Nashawtuc Architects Inc., Concord, MA.

p. 183: Photo: Charles Miller © The Taunton Press, Inc.; design: Sherri Buffa, Capstone Cabinetry and Design, Oakland, CA.

p. 184: Photos © davidduncanlivingston.com.

p. 185: Photo: Charles Bickford © The Taunton Press, Inc.; design: Dan Rockhill, Lawrence, KS.

p. 186: (top) Photo © Robert Perron; (bottom) photo © davidduncanlivingston.com.

p. 187: Photos: Charles Miller © The Taunton Press, Inc.; design: Kathryn Porter, Oakland, CA.

pp. 188–189: Photos: Charles Miller © The Taunton Press, Inc.

p. 190: Photo © davidduncanlivingston.com.

p. 191: (left) Photo: Charles Miller © The Taunton Press, Inc.; design: Jan Wisniewski, Santa Fe, NM; (right) photo © davidduncanlivingston.com.

p. 192: (left) Photo © davidduncanlivingston.com; (right) photo © Robert Perron; architect: Doug Williamson, Guilford, CT.

p. 193: Photos © Geoffrey Gross; design: Kaehler Moore Architects and Deborah T. Lipner, Ltd., both Greenwich, CT.

p. 194: Photo: Charles Miller © The Taunton Press, Inc.; design: Scott Stemper, architect, and Adam Turner, Dovetail Inc., General Contractors, both Seattle, WA.

p. 195: Photo © davidduncanlivingston.com.

p. 196: (left) Photo © davidduncanlivingston.com; (right) photo: Roe A. Osborn © The Taunton Press, Inc.; design: Pete and Connie di Girolamo; cabinetry: Glen Stewart.

p. 197: Photo © Robert Perron.

p. 198: Photo © davidduncanlivingston.com.

p. 199: (top) Photo © davidduncanlivingston.com; (bottom) photo ©Adrianne dePolo.

p. 200: (top left, right) Photos: Charles Miller © The Taunton Press, Inc.; design: Fu-Tung Cheng, Cheng Design, Berkeley, CA; (bottom) photo © davidduncanlivingston.com.

p. 201: Photo © Robert Benson.

p. 202: Photo: Roe A. Osborn © The Taunton Press, Inc.; design: Pete and Connie di Girolamo; cabinetry: Glen Stewart.

p. 203: (top) Photos: Roe A. Osborn © The Taunton Press, Inc.; design: Pete and Connie di Girolamo; cabinetry: Glen Stewart; (bottom) photo © davidduncanlivingston.com.

p. 204: Photos © davidduncanlivingston.com.

p. 205: Photo: Charles Miller © The Tunton Press, Inc.; design: Sherri Buffa, Capstone Cabinetry and Design, Oakland, CA.

p. 206: Photos © davidduncanlivingston.com.

p. 207: (top) Photo: Charles Miller © The Taunton Press, Inc.; design: Jim Garromone, Evanston, IL; (bottom) photos: Scott Gibson © The Taunton Press, Inc.; cabinetmaker: Serge Therrien, Sonoma, CA.

p. 208: Photos © davidduncanlivingston.com.

p. 209: (left) Photo: Charles Miller © The Taunton Press, Inc.; design: Fu-Tung Cheng, Cheng Design, Berkeley, CA; (right) photo © Geoffrey Gross; design: Kaehler Moore Associates and Deborah T. Lipner, Ltd., Greenwich, CT.

p. 210: (top left and right) Photos © davidduncanlivingston.com; (bottom) photo © Robert Perron.

p. 211: (top) Photo: Charles Miller © The Taunton Press, Inc.; cabinetmaker: Charles Chandler, Milwaukee, Wis.; (bottom) photo © Robert Perron; design: Strittmatter Kitchen and Baths.

p. 212: (top) Photo © Robert Perron; (bottom) photo: Charles Miller © The Taunton Press, Inc.; design: Keith Moskow, Boston, MA.

p. 213: Photo © davidduncanlivingston.com.

p. 214: (left) Photo © davidduncanlivingston.com; (right) photo: Charles Miller © The Taunton Press, Inc.; cabinetmaker: Charles Chandler, Milwaukee, WI.

p. 215: Photo © Robert Perron; design: Robert Orr Architects, New Haven, CT.

p. 216: (top) Photo © Randy O'Rourke; design: Austin Patterson Disston Architects, Southport, CT; (bottom) photo: Roe A. Osborn © The Taunton Press, Inc.; architect: William L. Burgin, Newport, RI.

p. 217: Photo © davidduncanlivingston.com.

p. 218: Photo © davidduncanlivingston.com.

p. 219: Photo: Charles Miller © The Taunton Press, Inc.

p. 220: (top) Photo: Roe A. Osborn © The Taunton Press, Inc.; design: William Rennie

Boyd, Santa Cruz, CA; (bottom) photo © Gabriel Benzur; design: Lou Ann Bauer, San Francisco, CA.

p. 221: Photo © John Kane; design: Austin Patterson Disston Architects, Southport, CT

p. 222: Photo © davidduncanlivingston.com.

p. 223: Photo © davidduncanlivingston.com; design: South Mountain Company, West Tisbury, MA.

p. 224: Photo © davidduncanlivingston.com.

p. 225: Photo © davidduncanlivingston.com.

p. 226: Photo © davidduncanlivingston.com; design: South Mountain Company, West Tisbury, MA.

p. 227: (top) Photo: Roe A. Osborn © The Taunton Press, Inc.; design: Mike Guertin, East Greenwich, RI; (bottom) photo: Charles Bickford © The Taunton Press, Inc.; design: Dan Rockhill, Lawrence, KS.

p. 228: (top) Photo © Susan Kahn; design: Liz and Rick O'Leary, Croton Falls, NY; (bottom) photo © Jerry Markatos; design: Dixon Weinstein Architects, Chapel Hill, NC.

p. 229 Photo: Kevin Ireton © The Taunton Press, Inc.; design: Thomas Lenchek, Balance Associates, Seattle, WA.

p. 230: (left) Photo © davidduncanlivingston.com; (right) photo © davidduncanlivingston.com; design: South Mountain Company, West Tisbury, MA.

p. 231: (left) Photo © davidduncanlivingston.com; (right) photo: Kevin Ireton © The Taunton Press, Inc.; design: Margaret Bakker and Rob Lewis,

Shavertown, PA, and builder Michael Millner, Pittsford, NY.

p. 232: (left) Photo © davidduncanlivingston.com; (right) photo © Derrill Bazzy; design: South Mountain Company, West Tisbury, MA.

p. 233: Photo © davidduncanlivingston.com.

p. 234: (top) Photo: Andy Engel © The Taunton Press, Inc.; design: Ernie Rose, Bon Air, VA; (bottom) photo © Ken Gutmaker; design: Austin Patterson Disston, Southport, CT.

p. 235: (top) Photo © Charles Register; design: Ellen Weinstein, Dixon Weinstein Architects, and Betsy West & Dee Blackburn, Chapel Hill, NC; (bottom) photo © davidduncanlivingston.com.

p. 236: Photo: Roe A. Osborn © The Taunton Press, Inc.; design: William Rennie Boyd, Santa Cruz, Calif.

p. 238: Photo: Andy Engel © The Taunton Press, Inc.; design: Brian Wormington.

p. 239: Photo © Charles Register; design: Dixon Weinstein Architects, Chapel Hill, NC.

p. 240: Photo © davidduncanlivingston.com.

p. 241: (top) Photo © Robert Perron; (bottom right) photo: Charles Miller © The Taunton Press, Inc.; design: David Edrington and Rob Thallon, Eugene, OR; (bottom left) photo: Charles Bickford © The Taunton Press, Inc.; design: Ron DiMauro and Glenn Sherman.

p. 242: Photo: Charles Miller © The Tunton Press, Inc.; design: Cathi and Steven House, House + House, San Francisco, CA.

p. 243: Photo © davidduncanlivingston.com.

p. 244: Photos © davidduncanlivingston.com.

p. 245: Photo © Durston Saylor.; design: Kaehler Moore Architects, Greenwich, CT.

p. 246: Photo © davidduncanlivingston.com.

p. 247: Photo © davidduncanlivingston.com.

p. 248: Photo: Charles Miller © The Taunton Press, Inc.; design: Eric Gazley.

p. 249: (left) Photo Charles Miller © The Taunton Press, Inc.; design: John and Nancy Carney, Jackson, WY.; (right) photo © davidduncanlivingston.com.

p. 251: Photos Andy Engel © The Taunton Press, Inc.; design (left): Ken Dahlin, Racine, WI; design (right): Brendan Coburn and parents, East Hampton, NY.

p. 252: Photos: Charles Miller © The Taunton Press, Inc.; design: Mac White, Michael G. Imber, Architect, San Antonio, TX.

p. 253: Photo © Randy O'Rourke; design: Austin Patterson Disston Architects, Southport, CT.

p. 254: Photo © davidduncanlivingston.com.

p. 255: (left) Photo: Scott Gibson © The Taunton Press, Inc.; (right) photo © davidduncanlivingston.com.

p. 256: Photo © Jerry Markatos; design: Dixon Weinstein Architects, Chapel Hill, NC.

p. 257: Photo © Joanne Kellar Bouknight; design: Norman Hoberman.

p. 258: Photo © Barry Halkin; design: Beardsley Architects, Philadelphia, PA.

p. 260: Photo © Randi Baird; design: South Mountain Company, West Tisbury, MA.

p. 261: (top) Photo © Derrill Bazzy; design: South Mountain Company, West Tisbury, MA; (bottom) photo © davidduncanlivingston.com; design: Andy Neumann, Carpenteria, CA.

p. 262: (top) Photo: Charles Bickford © The Taunton Press, Inc.; design: Mark Weber and Dan Wheeler, Wheeler Kearns Architects, Chicago, IL; (bottom) photo: Roe A. Osborn © The Taunton Press, Inc.; design: Gary M. Katz.

p. 263: Photos © Robert Perron; design: Elena Kalman, Greenwich, CT.

p. 264: Photo © Durston Saylor; design: Kaehler Moore Architects, Greenwich, CT.

p. 265: (left) Photo © Geoffrey Gross; design: Deborah T. Lipner Ltd., Greenwich, CT; (right) photo © davidduncanlivingston.com.

p. 266: Photo © davidduncanlivingston.com.

p. 267: Photo © Robert Perron; design: Killingworth.

p. 268: Photo: Roe A. Osborn © The Taunton Press, Inc.; design: William L. Burgin, Newport, RI.

p. 269: Photos: Charles Miller © The Taunton Press, Inc.; design: Robert B. Reed, Bellevue, WA.

p. 270: Photo © davidduncanlivingston.com.

p. 271: Photo © davidduncanlivingston.com; design: South Mountain Company, West Tisbury, MA.

p. 272: Photo: Kevin Ireton © The Taunton Press, Inc.; design: Tom Vermeland, Minneapolis, MN.

p. 273: Photo © Robert Perron; design: Mac Godley, New Canaan, CT.

p. 274: Photo © davidduncanlivingston.com.

p. 275: (top) Photo © Randi Baird; design: South Mountain Company, West Tisbury, MA; (bottom) photo © davidduncanlivingston.com.

p. 276: Photo: Roe A. Osborn © The Taunton Press, Inc.; design: Susan Aitcheson and Mike Guertin, East Greenwich, RI.

p. 278: Photo: Charles Bickford © The Taunton Press, Inc.; design: Patrick Camus.

p. 279: Photo © davidduncanlivingston.com.

p. 280: (top right) Photo © davidduncanlivingston.com; (bottom left) photo © davidduncanlivingston.com; design: Andy Neumann, Carpenteria, CA.

p. 281: (left) Photo © Charles Register; design: Dixon Weinstein Architects, Chapel Hill, NC; (right) photo © davidduncanlivingston.com.

p. 282: Photo © Durston Saylor; design: Kaehler Moore Architects, Greenwich, CT.

p. 283: (right) Photo: Kevin Ireton © The Taunton Press, Inc.; design: Tom Vermeland, Minneapolis, MN.

p. 284: (top) Photo © Durston Saylor; design: Kaehler Moore Architects, and Deborah T. Lipner, Ltd., both in Greenwich, CT; (bottom) photo © Barry Halkin; design: Christopher Beardsley, Philadelphia, PA.

p. 285: (top) Photos: Charles Miller © The Taunton Press, Inc.; design: Cathi and Steven House, House+ House, San Francisco, CA; (middle) photo © Robert Perron; design: Robert Knight, Blue Hill, ME.

p. 286: Photo © David Ericson; design: Dennis Parker, Honolulu, HI.

p. 287: (left) Photo © david-duncanlivingston.com; (right) photo © Randy O'Rourke; design: Kaehler Moore Architects, Greenwich, CT.

p. 288: (left) Photo © Robert Perron; (top right) photo © Randy O'Rourke; design: Kaehler Moore Architects, Greenwich, CT; (bottom right) photo: Charles Miller © The Taunton Press, Inc.; design: Helen Degenhardt, Berkeley, CA.

p. 289: (left) Photo Charles Miller © The Taunton Press, Inc.; design: John and Nancy Carney, Jackson, WY.; (right) photo © Randy O'Rourke; design: Austin Patterson Disston, Southport, CT.

p. 290-291: Photos © Susan Kahn; design: Liz and Rick O'Leary, Croton Falls, NY.

p. 292: (left) Photo © david-duncanlivingston.com; (right) photo © Durston Saylor; design: Kaehler Moore Architects, Greenwich, CT.

p. 293: Photos: Roe A. Osborn © The Taunton Press, Inc.; design: Pete di Girolamo, Salerno, Livingston Architects, San Diego, CA; ceramic design: Connie di Girolamo; cabinetry: Glen Stewart, San Diego, CA.

p. 294: Photo: Charles Miller © The Taunton Press, Inc.; design: Beth Coleman, Ellison Bay, WI.

p. 295: (left) Photo: Charles Bickford © The Taunton Press, Inc.; design: Dale Brentrup, Charlotte, NC; (right) photo: Kevin Ireton © The Taunton Press, Inc.; design: Michael Millner, Pittsford, NY.

p. 296: Photo © davidduncanlivingston.com; (right) photo: Charles Miller © The Taunton Press, Inc.; design: Kurt Lavenson, Alamo, CA.

p. 297: (left) Photo: Scott Gibson © The Taunton Press, Inc.; design: William F. Roslansky, Woods Hole, Mass.; (right) photo © Durston Saylor; design: Kaehler Moore Architects, Greenwich, CT.

p. 298: Photo: Kevin Ireton © The Taunton Press, Inc.; design: Tom Vermeland, Minneapolis, MN; (right) photo © Tom O'Brien; design: furniture maker: Bryce Ritter, Skippack, PA; architect: Louis A. DiBerardino, New Canaan, CT.

p. 299: Photo © Durston Saylor; design: Kaehler Moore Architects, and Deborah T. Lipner, Ltd., both in Greenwich, CT.

p. 300: Photo © Susan Kahn; design: Liz and Rick O'Leary, Croton Falls, NY.

p. 301: (top left) Photo © davidduncanlivingston.com; (bottom left) photo © Randi Baird; design: South Mountain Company, Martha's Vineyard, MA; (right) photo © Zachary Gaulkin; design: Stephen Lauziere.